THE CAPTIVE

Photograph by Florence Vandamm

MISS HELEN MENKEN AS IRENE DE MONTCEL

THE CAPTIVE

BY

EDOUARD BOURDET

Translated from the French by

ARTHUR HORNBLOW, Jr.

Introduction by

J. BROOKS ATKINSON

WILDSIDE PRESS

Published - - October, 1926
Second Printing, November, 1926
Third Printing, December, 1926
Fourth Printing, March, 1927
Fifth Printing, March, 1927

MANUFACTURED IN THE UNITED STATES OF AMERICA

TO

GILBERT MILLER

WHOSE SPLENDID PRODUCTION OF THIS PLAY HAS EARNED THE ADMIRATION AND GRATITUDE OF THE AUTHOR AND HIS TRANSLATOR

INTRODUCTION

During the summer and early autumn of 1926, rumors that an American producer was bringing to America an adaptation of Bourdet's "La Prisonnière" were received with a good deal of uncertainty by the more responsible citizens of New York. For the theatrical news from Paris, where this trenchant drama began its career, had stressed the audacity of the theme, with a general tintinnabulation about censorship and the decadence of the stage. And those who were already nauseated by the fetid smells of several plays then current were quite naturally distressed at the prospect of sensationalism in the form of abnormality. Surely, they complained, themes of this character are not fit subjects for open portrayal on the stage. Indeed, the audience assembled for the opening performance at the Empire Theatre was obviously prepared for a violent shock. But whatever the expectations may have been, the objective treatment of the theme and the austere quality of the performance cleared the humid air like a northwestern breeze. With Mr. Hornblow's adaptation and Mr. Miller's masterly direction "The Captive" became, as it was written, a restrained though uncompromising tragedy, rather than a malodorous truckling to low curiosity. Thus for the thousandth time it was evident that the motives of a dramatic production are of far greater importance than the details of the subject-matter.

Not that M. Bourdet has cloaked his drama under the sanctimony of the crusader's armor. If one may judge by the haunting impression left by the grim performance, M. Bourdet is interested, not in the details of his theme, but in their illumination of human character; and he is by that sign pre-eminently a dramatist. None of the soul-flagellations of a Rousseau or a Strindberg alleviates the horror by distributing the blame among gods and men, or by sighing over the sensual temptations or the squalor. Choosing a Greek theme M. Bourdet treats of it, if not in the classical manner, then in the modern counterpart to that tragic inevitability. In fine, the play approaches its subject objectively. And since M. Bourdet understands his characters through and through, his conclusion is foreordained. In reading it we have no feeling that he is shaping it to prove an arbitrary thesis, or to lead his characters through theatrical adventures for lurid effects. So "The Captive" moves swiftly through three long acts; even before the nature of the malady is defined in the second act, doom swims over the play like a thick, black cloud.

Although, as the reader will soon discover, the occasion for "The Captive" is the fact of an abnormal relationship between two women, the interest is solely in its revelation of character. M. Bourdet has described his people as ordinary well-bred human beings, whatever their failings may be. Irene's tenderness towards her little sister, and her own humility and anguish, reveal her as a young lady of fine instincts; she is in no sense the neurotic debauchee of tawdry melodrama. Jacques Virieu, likewise, is a young man of high impulses; and of sufficient strength of character to fly recklessly in the face of danger to support an ideal. Unlike the contemporary school of pettifogging novelists and dramatists, with their garish sophistication, M. Bourdet does not excuse his characters on the score of congenital weakness or worldly disillusionment or pseudo-scientific buncombe. No, indeed, he is not interested in excuses; his is a tragedy of consequences. He shows Irene estranged from her father, playing false to her ingenuous sister, and fast losing all the friends with whom she once associated freely. He tortures her before Jacques. Once she was his ideal, a woman to whom he looked up; now she comes as a petitioner for mercy and pity rather than respect. In the second act, M. Bourdet shows the husband of the unseen Madame d'Aiguines—a simulacrum of a man, gray before his time, wretched and tormented, unable to escape from a poisoned home. All these characters, involved in various ways, have been withered a little by their proximity to the festered one. And if any proof were needed of the sincerity of M. Bourdet's purpose, his treatment of Madame d'Aiguines would be sufficient. They talk of her occasionally, but by keeping her in the background and by describing the blighted fruits of her influence, M. Bourdet retains the fine objectivity and austerity of his drama.

M. Bourdet casts his tragedy in the familiar three-act mold of crisp, economical playwrighting. Without bothering his head too much about details of craftsmanship, without wasting time over the motivation of exits and entrances, he pursues his course vigorously to the end. As the composer contrasts his main theme with fragile, minor developments, so M. Bourdet heightens his tragedy by rippling interludes with Gisele and Françoise Meillant, fresh, charming and frank. This is M. Bourdet's first notable play; he is still in his thirties. His first play was "Le Rubicon," put on at the Théâtre Michel in 1910. During the war M. Bourdet abandoned his career as a playwright to fight in the infantry; he was wounded twice, cited three times for bravery, and given the cross of the Legion of Honor. In the trenches he met as a fellow officer a young man who was deliberately seeking death in battle as an escape from the wretchedness of his home life. This man corresponds to the d'Aiguines of "The Captive," and was the germ of the present play. The planning and writing of the tragedy occupied M. Bourdet off and on for two years. Within a year after its first appearance in Paris, "The Captive" was played in Berlin, Vienna, Budapest and New York. Mr. Hornblow's notable adaptation communicates the precise flavor of the original.

J. Brooks Atkinson.

October, 1926.

LA PRISONNIÈRE by Edouard Bourdet was presented for the first time on any stage at the Théâtre Femina in Paris on March 6th, 1926. Adapted by Arthur Hornblow, Jr., it was presented for the first time in English under the title of THE CAPTIVE at the Empire Theatre in New York, on September 29th, 1926. The play was presented by the Charles Frohman Company and produced by Gilbert Miller with the following cast:

DE MONTCEL .... NORMAN TREVOR
IRENE DE MONTCEL .... HELEN MENKEN
GISELE DE MONTCEL .... ANN TREVOR
JACQUES VIRIEU .... BASIL RATHBONE
D'AIGUINES .... ARTHUR WONTNER
FRANÇOISE MEILLANT .... ANN ANDREWS
MLLE. MARCHAND .... WINIFRED FRASER
JOSEPHINE .... MINNA PHILLIPS
GEORGES .... ARTHUR LEWIS

THE CAPTIVE

THE CHARACTERS

De Montcel
Irene de Montcel
Gisele de Montcel
Jacques Virieu
D'Aiguines
Françoise Meillant
Mlle. Marchand
Josephine
Georges

Act I: Irene de Montcel's room in her father's apartment; Paris.
Act II: Jacques Virieu's study. One month later.
Act III: The same. A year later.

THE CAPTIVE

ACT ONE

SCENE: IRENE'S *room in her father's apartment, Paris. A door at the left leads to a dressing room; another in back gives onto the hall, a third at the right connects with* GISELE'S *room.*

The room is furnished simply but with period pieces of uncommon taste; the bed lies in a recess, there is a small divan, some comfortable chairs and a table. On the latter stands a telephone.

On the walls hang several photographic copies of paintings of the Italian school. In the far corner stands an artist's easel, faced toward the wall.

When the curtain rises the room is empty; then the door at the right half opens and GISELE, *an attractive girl of seventeen, looks in.*

GISELE

[*Calls*]: Irene? [*She enters and proceeds to the door at left*] Irene? [*Looking off*] She's not there. [MLLE. MARCHAND, GISELE'S *governess, enters at right.*]

MLLE. MARCHAND

I told you she hadn't come in yet. It's only six o'clock . . . that's much too early for her.

GISELE

But she told me she'd be back early to-night because of the dinner. She's supposed to help me fix the flowers for the table.

MLLE. MARCHAND

I wouldn't count on her too much if I were you. Would you like me to help you?

GISELE

Oh, I'd rather she did. If I do them without her they won't look like anything.

MLLE. MARCHAND

Very well.

GISELE

Isn't she tiresome always being late like this! What *am* I to do about my dress?

MLLE. MARCHAND

What about it?

GISELE

I've got to know what dress to put on!

MLLE. MARCHAND

Surely you don't need your sister to decide that?

GISELE

Well, you see we're the only two women at dinner to-night, and we must arrange that our dresses don't clash.

MLLE. MARCHAND

Ah, yes, that's so.

[JOSEPHINE, *a maid, enters at the back, carrying a gown to be put away in the dressing room.*]

GISELE

Josephine, has Irene told you what dress she's wearing to-night?

JOSEPHINE

No, mademoiselle, she hasn't.

GISELE

Oh, Lord! Now I've no idea what to wear myself! [JOSEPHINE *goes out.*]

MLLE. MARCHAND

Wear your yellow dress. It's charming—and it's very becoming.

GISELE

My yellow dress! Don't be silly!

MLLE. MARCHAND

Gisele! A little more respect for your governess, if you please!

GISELE

I'm sorry, mademoiselle. I respect you, dear,—but when it comes to clothes I must say you don't know what you're talking about!

MLLE. MARCHAND

But what have you got against the yellow dress?

GISELE

Much too formal! It's just a little political dinner . . . papa said the men won't dress. We'll be only eight in all . . . a few antiques from the Foreign Office . . . and a couple of senators. It'll be a regular wilderness of whiskers!

MLLE. MARCHAND

Gisele! If you please!

GISELE

What's the matter?

MLLE. MARCHAND

If you're not a bit more careful in your language, you'll never get along in Rome, my dear. Please remember that you're to be very nearly an official personage there. The daughter of an ambassador is somebody. Every word of yours will be noticed and criticized, you may be sure.

GISELE

[*Smiling*]: Nonsense!

[M. DE MONTCEL *appears at the back. He is a tall, distinguished looking man of fifty.*]

MONTCEL

Is Irene here?

GISELE

No, papa, she's not in yet.

MONTCEL

[*Half to himself*]: Naturally! [*Aloud.*] Good evening, mademoiselle. Don't get up. [*To* GISELE.] Please see that I'm told the moment she gets in.

GISELE

Very well, papa.

[MONTCEL *starts to go.*]

GISELE

Papa?

MONTCEL

Yes?

GISELE

If it's about the dinner that you want to see Irene, you might tell me. . . .

MONTCEL

No, it's not about the dinner.

GISELE

Oh.

MONTCEL

Have her inform me as soon as she comes in, won't you. . . . Even if I have some one with me in the study.

GISELE

Yes, papa.

[MONTCEL *goes out.*]

So! The storm's ready to break! Well, I felt it coming!

MLLE. MARCHAND

Is there something the matter between Irene and your father?

GISELE

Why, they haven't said a word to each other for over a week. "Good morning" "Good evening." That's all. Oh, it'll be jolly in Rome if things go on like this! At least here, papa is away three days out of four. But in Rome . . .

MLLE. MARCHAND

What's the quarrel about?

GISELE

Ah! That's a mystery! [*Pause.*] Do you remember a few days ago after luncheon . . . when Irene asked papa if she might speak to him alone . . . in his study?

MLLE. MARCHAND

Yes, I remember.

GISELE

It all began then. I've no idea what they said to each other. I tried to get it out of Irene but couldn't. She told me not to worry about it and that it would all come out all right. Then she changed the subject. . . . I saw it was no use insisting.

MLLE. MARCHAND

Do you think it's because your father was vexed with Irene for having refused that young man?

GISELE

What young man?

MLLE. MARCHAND

The young man your aunt introduced here. You know perfectly well.

GISELE

Oh, good heavens, no! That's ancient history . . . why, it was over a month ago. No, no—that's been forgotten. Anyhow, that makes the third suitor that Irene's refused this year so I suppose papa's beginning to get used to it. No, it's something else.

MLLE. MARCHAND

Perhaps your father's beginning to notice that Irene leads a rather—rather odd life for a young unmarried girl.

GISELE

Oh, hullo! Back to the old subject! It's a long time since you've complained about Irene's behavior.

MLLE. MARCHAND

I'm not—complaining, my dear. In the first place it's not my concern . . . no longer my concern, at any rate, thank heaven. If I were still responsible for her bringing up I might complain—and for good reason. But fortunately I'm not.

GISELE

Oh, come on,—surely you don't expect that at twenty-five Irene should lead the same existence I do at seventeen?

MLLE. MARCHAND

Why not? The elder Robien girl is twenty-four and her sister eighteen. Yet they lead precisely the same lives; they go about only with their mother or their companion.

GISELE

I hope you're not trying to compare that pill Valentine Robien with Irene!

MLLE. MARCHAND

They're girls of the same age and same class as you.

GISELE

You know perfectly well that Irene isn't anything like them!

MLLE. MARCHAND

And why not, pray?

GISELE

Do you know many girls as brilliant—as cultured—as attractive as Irene?

MLLE. MARCHAND

What of it?

GISELE

Well, certainly you can't expect a girl like that to spend her life in a nursery—with a kid sister and a wet nurse! She'd be bored to death!

MLLE. MARCHAND

I don't know whether she'd be bored to death as you so tactfully put it . . . but I *do* know it would be far better for her reputation than spending every minute away from home and alone . . . without ever telling any one where she goes.

GISELE

What do you mean, "where she goes"? She goes to the studio, to her teacher. She works at her painting.

MLLE. MARCHAND

Very well.

GISELE

You don't believe that?

MLLE. MARCHAND

Yes, I believe it, my dear. I'm sure of it, but nevertheless it's no life for a girl of good family. You can't change my mind as to that. It's not the way to find a good husband.

GISELE

When it comes to that you needn't worry about Irene. The day she wants to—

MLLE. MARCHAND

The day she wants to may be too late. However, it's not my affair. It's your father's.

GISELE

Oh, as for papa's bothering! . . . [*Pause.*] Naturally, he'd prefer to see us both married so as to be rid of us,—and then he could take *all* his meals at Madame de Vallon's. He'd love that!

MLLE. MARCHAND

Gisele! You will kindly not speak in that way of your father!

GISELE

What have I said? It's entirely within papa's rights to prefer Madame de Vallon's cook to ours. It seems that she has a superb cook! I really can't conceive how papa will do without that cook in Rome! . . . Perhaps he'll take her there—as he did to Brussels. Do you think he will?

MLLE. MARCHAND

Gisele!

GISELE

The *cook*, I mean!

MLLE. MARCHAND

Gisele, will you be still! The subject is not a proper one!

GISELE

All right! Don't be cross. I'll be still. [*She kisses* MLLE. MARCHAND, *laughingly.*] Poor mademoiselle! [*The door at the back opens and* IRENE *enters. She is smartly dressed and wears a bunch of violets.* GISELE *goes toward her gayly*]: Ah, there you are!

IRENE

[*Somewhat seriously; with the air of one who has something on her mind*]: What are you doing in here, you two?

GISELE

Waiting for you. Know what time it is?

IRENE

Yes, I'm late. I couldn't find a taxi.

GISELE

Tell me,—what dress are you going to wear to-night?

IRENE

What dress?

MLLE. MARCHAND

Gisele, don't forget your father's message to Irene.

GISELE

Oh, yes; papa said that you were to notify him the minute you got in.

IRENE

Oh.

GISELE

He said to let him know even if there were people in with him.

IRENE

[*As though to herself*]: Very well.

GISELE

Shall I tell him?

IRENE

Yes—if you don't mind.

MLLE. MARCHAND

[*To* GISELE]: Well, I'll say good night, my dear. It's after six. I must go home.

GISELE

Do wait a moment. I'll be right back. [*She runs out at back.*]

[IRENE *in a thoughtful mood removes her hat and cloak and puts them on a chair.*]

MLLE. MARCHAND

Well, Irene, how are you getting on with your painting? Are you satisfied?

IRENE

[*Inattentive*]: What? . . . Oh, yes, thank you, mademoiselle.

MLLE. MARCHAND

Are you making headway?

IRENE

Slowly, yes.

MLLE. MARCHAND

It still interests you very much, does it?

IRENE

Oh, yes, it still does. [*She puts her violets on the table. There is an awkward moment of silence.* GISELE *returns.*]

GISELE

Papa says he'll come in here.

IRENE

Very well.

MLLE. MARCHAND

Good night, Irene.

IRENE

Good night, mademoiselle. [*They shake hands.*]

MLLE. MARCHAND

[*To* GISELE, *kissing her*]: Till to-morrow, dear.

GISELE

[*Seeing her to the door*]: I've an Italian lesson at two. So will you come at about three?

MLLE. MARCHAND

At about three. . . .

GISELE

We can take a walk through the park if it's fine. . . .

[*They go out.* GISELE *returns almost at once. To* IRENE]: You haven't told me what dress you're going to wear?

IRENE

I don't know, dear. Whichever you prefer; it doesn't matter to me.

GISELE

Then wear your white, do you mind? I'll wear my blue,—you know, the new one, to try it out.

IRENE

All right. Tell me, dear, do you know why father wants to see me?

GISELE

No. I asked him if it were something about the dinner, but he said no. That's all I can tell you.

IRENE

What mood is he in?

GISELE

A little stern. But that means nothing . . . he's so often that way.

[MONTCEL *appears at the back.*]

MONTCEL

Gisele, would you mind leaving us, child. I wish to speak with Irene.

GISELE

Yes, papa.

[*She goes into her room and closes the door.*]

MONTCEL

[*After a pause*]: I might begin, my dear, by saying that what we have to discuss is extremely serious. My attitude toward you from now on must depend upon it. Before making any decision I wanted to give you ample time to think things over. Have you done so?

IRENE

Yes, father.

MONTCEL

Well? Then tell me what conclusion you've reached.

IRENE

I have not changed my mind, father.

MONTCEL

Which means?

IRENE

That I still ask you to let me stay here when you leave for Rome.

MONTCEL

So! This past week has gone for nothing. You persist in asking me something which you know perfectly well is impossible.

IRENE

I persist in asking it. But I cannot see that it's impossible.

MONTCEL

Very well. You also persist in withholding the reason for your extraordinary request.

IRENE

I've already given it to you, father.

MONTCEL

You've told me you wished to remain in Paris because of your work, your painting. That's it, isn't it?

IRENE

Exactly.

MONTCEL

Irene,—consider well, my child, what I'm asking you. Will you or will you not give me the true reason?

IRENE

There is no other.

MONTCEL

[*Irritated*]: Come, come, this is childish! If it were a question of your going to live on a desert island your excuse might take on the semblance of truth. But it's a question of your living in Rome, in the heart of Italy, the very cradle of art. Why, only last year you didn't stop begging me to let you go there,—and once you'd gone I had the devil's own time getting you to come back! [*Pause.*] Of course, it's true that it was there that you made the acquaintance of those people—those d'Aiguines—who since then seem to have become the very center of your existence.

IRENE

What have Monsieur and Madame d'Aiguines to do with this?

MONTCEL

Perhaps it's I who might ask you that. But I'll limit myself to saying that I deplore your constant association with them.

IRENE

Why?

MONTCEL

It is not a fit one for you.

IRENE

But what have you against them?

MONTCEL

Many things. To begin with, it's not to his credit that he had to leave the diplomatic service at the time of his marriage.

IRENE

Because he married a foreigner.

MONTCEL

An Austrian, I know.

IRENE

Well, then. . . .

MONTCEL

If you don't mind, let's put aside the subject of the d'Aiguines. Let's get back to Rome, where as I was saying, you'll be in an excellent position to keep on with your painting.

IRENE

When one starts with a certain teacher it's not wise to change. Mine is not in Rome, he is here.

MONTCEL

Do you work a great deal with your teacher?

IRENE

Of course.

MONTCEL

Every day, I suppose?

IRENE

Practically, yes.

MONTCEL

That's not true.

IRENE

What?

MONTCEL

I've been to see your teacher.

IRENE

You've been to see him?

MONTCEL

To-day. I wanted to satisfy myself. I went to ask him if he were pleased with his pupil. I left his studio fully aware of the real place that painting occupies in your life.

IRENE

What did he tell you?

MONTCEL

That he had not seen you at his studio for a month!

IRENE

[*Faltering*]: I've been making a copy at the Louvre.

MONTCEL

Really! Well, in that case, my child, you have cause to be very pleased, for in Rome you'll find galleries where you'll be able to copy some of the most beautiful pictures in the world.

IRENE

Why are you so insistent that I come with you?

MONTCEL

Because the place of a young unmarried woman is with her family and because until you *are* married your family is your father . . . even if at times you appear to forget it.

IRENE

If I forget it, father, perhaps it's because you don't always remember it yourself.

MONTCEL

What do you mean by that?

IRENE

Oh, nothing. . . .

MONTCEL

Excuse me. . . . I insist that you explain your remark.

IRENE

If a daughter's place is with her father why did you never think of having us join you while you were in Brussels?

MONTCEL

I've already told you it was because of my quarters there.

IRENE

Only because of that, I suppose?

MONTCEL

[*With growing temper*]: Which of us two owes explanations to the other? You or I? Let that be enough. You are free to think of me what you wish; it makes no difference. But I am your father and I intend to exact obedience from you. [*Forcibly.*] I had thought until now that you were a serious-minded girl, well able to conduct herself properly . . . I have treated you accordingly. I was mistaken. I shall treat you in the future as you deserve. I shall leave for Rome as soon as my successor arrives here, which will be early next month. You and your sister will leave with me.

IRENE

[*Softly*]: No, father.

MONTCEL

What do you say?

IRENE

I shall not leave. I have already told you so.

MONTCEL

[*Thoroughly angered*]: You shall leave! You'll go or be *forced* to go!

IRENE

[*Willfully*]: As to that! . . .

MONTCEL

Take care, Irene. You should know me well enough to realize that when I've made up my mind to something it's dangerous to oppose me. I've broken stronger wills than yours in my career.

IRENE

And you should know me, father. I'm your daughter, and in that respect we are alike.

MONTCEL

Enough! I'll not tolerate your threats!

IRENE

[*Controls herself*]: They are not threats. But I'm twenty-five. I'm no longer a child and you must realize that I wouldn't have come to you the other day as I did if I had not also made up my mind.

MONTCEL

Made up your mind to what—remain in Paris?

IRENE

Yes.

MONTCEL

Where do you intend to live?

IRENE

Why—here.

MONTCEL

Oh, no, not here. I'm very sorry, but I've decided to sublet the apartment. It costs a great deal, and I'll have no reason for holding on to it after leaving Paris.

IRENE

Oh.

MONTCEL

That being the case, may I ask where you expect to go?

IRENE

Well . . . to an hotel, I suppose.

MONTCEL

And how will you support yourself? With what money? Not with mine. You'll not have a penny from me.

IRENE

But, father. . . .

MONTCEL

Not a penny, let that be clear! As long as I live! . . . and I might inform you—at the risk of disappointing you—that the present state of my health gives no cause for alarm. [*Pause.*] That offers a new side to the question, eh?

IRENE

If you think you can force your will on me in any such way as that—

MONTCEL

If that way fails, there are others.

IRENE

What others?

MONTCEL

I'll tell you. Not only you'll never have a penny of mine but so far as I'm concerned you'll no longer exist. I shall never see you again. I realize that's probably the least of your worries. Your affection for me will readily bear that separation. But what may cause you more concern is to learn that I shall never again let you see your sister.

IRENE

[*Dismayed*]: Oh!

MONTCEL

Never!

IRENE

You'd do that?

MONTCEL

Most assuredly.

IRENE

It's wicked of you!

MONTCEL

Wicked or not, my plain duty is to guard her against you. I shall do so, believe me.

IRENE

Guard her against me! Do you know what you're

saying, father? What would become of the poor child without me. Who'd take care of her? I'm all she has in the world.

MONTCEL

Really! I don't count, I suppose!

IRENE

You—oh, but father . . .

MONTCEL

I what? Come, come, finish your thought. She doesn't love me, is that it? She doesn't love me any more than you do!

IRENE

[*Quietly*]: And you, father . . . do you love us? Have you ever given us a moment's concern, a moment's bother? I may as well say it, since we're on the subject. What has our childhood been? Not a happy one, father. Always alone with servants. If Gisele hadn't had me and I her, there'd have been little enough affection in our lives since mother's death.

MONTCEL

You're beginning that over again, eh?

IRENE

No, father. . . . It's finished. . . . You've done what you wanted to. It isn't for us to attempt to judge you. But, if after having accustomed us to be everything to each other for fifteen years, you think to separate us, you're mistaken, that's all.

MONTCEL

If that's the case, tell me,—since you believe yourself so necessary to your sister—how can you consider remaining here while she's in Rome? Eh,—tell me *that?*

IRENE

Why shouldn't she also stay here?

MONTCEL

With you? In your care? Are you quite mad? You don't really believe that I could trust that child to you. To *you!* That's superb!

IRENE

What do you mean?

MONTCEL

I mean that your sister is a sweet, innocent girl. I propose that she shall remain so! Now you have it!

IRENE

Oh! Father! . . .

MONTCEL

I'm sorry, but I must say what I think,—what your behavior compels me to think. If I'm wrong you have only to justify yourself.

IRENE

There is no need for me to justify myself.

MONTCEL

God in heaven! If the reason you had for wishing to remain here were the kind that a daughter might tell her father, you'd have let me hear it long ago.

IRENE

I have told you it was my painting.

MONTCEL

[*Gazing steadily at her*]: I had thought you more intelligent than this. As things stand now I'd tell the truth if I were you. It would be better.
[IRENE *is silent.*]

You don't want to? Don't you see that your silence is the most damning evidence against you? Do you think that with what I already take for granted and what I may guess it will still be difficult for me to find out the rest?

IRENE

What do you take for granted?

MONTCEL

You'd like to know?

IRENE

Yes.

MONTCEL

I take for granted that since you don't wish to come to Rome there is some one who holds you here. That's what I think! Am I not right? . . . Answer me!

[*She is silent.*]

Listen, Irene. . . . I'm determined to throw full light on this matter, do you understand? By keeping up this silence you will simply force me to take unpleasant steps which you can still prevent.

IRENE

What steps?

MONTCEL

Never mind! But I promise you I'll get at the truth. I'll insist upon it in a place where I know I can find it and where there'll be no evading it.

IRENE

Where?

MONTCEL

From those whom I must suppose are acquainted with the intimate facts of your life. Your devoted friends the d'Aiguines.

IRENE

[*Thunderstruck*]: That's mad, father!

MONTCEL

I think not.

IRENE

But—whatever gave you the idea—of asking the d'Aiguines about such a thing?

MONTCEL

The idea occurred to me after certain things I've observed.

IRENE

What have you observed?

MONTCEL

I must be allowed to keep that to myself for the present.

IRENE

But at least I have the right to know?—

MONTCEL

No, you have not! [*Pause.*] You seem curiously disturbed that I should take this step.

IRENE

I,—not at all! It's a matter of complete indifference to me.

MONTCEL

Really? Why, then, were you so agitated by my mention of the name d'Aiguines?

IRENE

[*Disturbed*]: I wasn't agitated

MONTCEL

You were! Besides, it's very simple. [*Looks at his watch.*] We'll settle this right away.

IRENE

What are you going to do?

MONTCEL

Ask Monsieur d'Aiguines to come here and have a talk with me immediately.

IRENE

You won't do that, father!

MONTCEL

You'll see.

IRENE

Even if I tell you that it would be quite useless, that you will learn nothing?

MONTCEL

Ah! So you're already beginning to admit things! Listen,—listen to me—if within two minutes you have not spoken the name I wish to hear, I shall ask d'Aiguines for it whether you wish me to or not!

IRENE

Father, I beg you not to do this!

MONTCEL

Then tell me. On whose account do you wish to remain in Paris? Will you tell me,—yes or no?

IRENE

[*In despair*]: But, father—

MONTCEL

[*After a moment*]: All right, I'm through! [*He reaches the door, back.*]

IRENE

[*Imploringly*]: Father! No, father!

MONTCEL

[*At door*]: Well?

IRENE

It's on account—of—Jacques.

Photograph by Florence Vandamm

MONTCEL: Listen,—Listen to me—if within two minutes you have not spoken the name I wish to hear, I shall ask d'Aiguines for it—whether you wish me to or not!

(HELEN MENKEN *and* NORMAN TREVOR)

MONTCEL

[*Surprised*]: Jacques? Jacques who? Jacques Virieu?

IRENE

Yes.

MONTCEL

[*Still surprised*]: It's on account of Jacques that you want to remain in Paris?

IRENE

[*Nervously*]: Well,—yes.

MONTCEL

Upon my soul! [*Pause.*] What's going on between you two?

IRENE

Nothing.

MONTCEL

What do you mean, nothing?

IRENE

Nothing serious, I assure you.

MONTCEL

Would you mind not juggling words with me. I warn you that all you say will be verified.

IRENE

Of course, father.

MONTCEL

So I advise you not to try to hide anything from me. Now, answer my question. What is going on between you?

IRENE

[*With difficulty*]: We've been fond of each other for some time and we had thought,—at least, *I* had thought that I might marry him,—that's all.

MONTCEL

You're telling me everything?

IRENE

Yes.

MONTCEL

So you and Jacques want to get married?

IRENE

I said that *I* wanted to,—that is, I'd like to.

MONTCEL

And he?

IRENE

I don't know.

MONTCEL

Do you mean to say he hasn't spoken of his intentions?

IRENE

No.

MONTCEL

Then how do things stand?

IRENE

He hasn't spoken yet.

MONTCEL

And you imagine that he's getting ready to? Eh? Speak! Explain yourself . . . don't make me force every word out of you!

IRENE

I'm not certain of anything.

MONTCEL

Then, as I understand it, you love him . . . if he were to propose you'd be inclined to say yes. Is that it?

IRENE

[*After a pause*]: Yes.

MONTCEL

And it's with this hope in mind that you'd prefer remaining in Paris?

IRENE

Yes.

MONTCEL

Well, for heaven's sake, my dear, why haven't you simply said so instead of keeping up this air of mystery?

IRENE

It wasn't my secret alone.

MONTCEL

Why, it isn't betraying a secret of that kind to tell it to one's father. Besides you must have known perfectly well that there's nothing about your idea that displeases me. Jacques's a distant relative of ours on his mother's side. . . . You've known each other since you were children . . . he goes with the same sort of people we do. He's a fine boy, and I'm very fond of him. To make things complete his electrical concession in Morocco assures him a good income. There's no possible reason for my opposing your wish.

IRENE

I didn't want to tell you about something which may exist only in my imagination.

MONTCEL

Why not? Where's the harm?

IRENE

Well, it's not exactly pleasant having to confess oneself mistaken about a thing like that. You must understand.

MONTCEL

We must learn to pocket our pride at times. Instead of being afraid of me you should have looked upon me as your natural guide and adviser. I realize that *you* can't ask the young man to reveal the state of his feelings; that wouldn't be quite the thing. But *I* can do it easily, without your pride being hurt in any way.

IRENE

But father, that's impossible! . . .

MONTCEL

It's so far from being impossible, my dear, that I'll prove it by taking the matter up with Jacques to-morrow.

IRENE

You don't really mean to!

MONTCEL

Don't worry. . . . I'll leave you out of it. I'll not even refer to our conversation,—

IRENE

But, father. . . .

MONTCEL

[*Going on*]: . . . I'll merely tell him that for some time past a number of things have led me to believe that you were developing a deep affection for some one. That I have watched you closely and come to understand, without your saying a word, that your feelings concerned him. I'll then say that, as I'm about to leave Paris to be gone for some time, I'd like to know if he has anything to say to me. Just that.

IRENE

Father, I beg you to do nothing of the sort. . . !

MONTCEL

I'm sorry to oppose your wishes, my dear, but under the circumstances I'm a better judge of what should be done than you. Some day you'll thank me for it.

IRENE

I don't want you to do it!

MONTCEL

Do you prefer going to Rome without knowing what he—?

IRENE

I prefer to wait, without rushing matters.

MONTCEL

Wait for what? For him to make up his mind? Don't forget that I'm leaving in three weeks' time.

IRENE

Well, naturally, we can't expect things to develop much in three weeks.

MONTCEL

Well, then?

IRENE

That's exactly why I want to stay behind.

MONTCEL

Under no conditions! Unless, of course, he has proposed formally, and even then . . . we'll see.

IRENE

But you've just said you had faith in him.

MONTCEL

No. Don't insist. It's quite useless. I shall speak to him, just as I've outlined and—

IRENE

Father, please!

MONTCEL

Don't be afraid. I'll talk with him as man to man in the friendliest possible way. Whatever his sentiments may be he won't be able to take any exception to what is said.

IRENE

For the last time, father, I beg you not to do this!

MONTCEL

That's enough, my child. My mind is made up and I shan't change it. Let's leave it at that for this evening if you don't mind. It's already half past six and I must run around to the Foreign Office before dinner. [*He goes toward the door, back.*] By the bye, will you put Dardennes at your right and Couvreur at your left. Dinner's at eight-fifteen. [*He goes out.*]

[IRENE *seems tremendously disturbed as soon as she is alone. She drops into a chair, musing; then suddenly rising, goes to her table and lifts the telephone receiver.*]

IRENE

[*Into the telephone*]: Elysèes 24-51 . . . Please. Hullo? . . . Elysèes 24-51? . . . May I speak to

Monsieur Jacques Virieu? Oh, it's you, Jacques? I didn't recognize your voice. . . . You knew mine? . . . I'm glad. Listen, Jacques, is there any way of my seeing you? . . . Yes—if you wish. . . . But wouldn't it be possible right away? . . . Could you come here? . . . Thanks so much. I'll expect you. . . . What? . . . Oh, I'll tell you, I can't over the telephone. . . . Good-by!

[*She replaces the receiver, and for a moment remains pensively where she is.* GISELE *enters at right.*]

GISELE

May I come in?

IRENE

Certainly, dear. Dressed so soon?

GISELE

But it's fairly late. And we haven't fixed the flowers yet.

IRENE

Oh! please do it without me. I simply won't have the time. [IRENE *goes to dressing room.*]

GISELE

All right. They'll be too awful, but what's the difference?

IRENE

[*From dressing room*]: Of course they won't. Don't be silly! . . . Ring for Josephine, dear, do you mind? I must dress.

GISELE

[*Rings bell.*] Irene?

IRENE

What, darling?

JOSEPHINE

[*Entering at the back, to* GISELE]: Did you ring, mademoiselle?

GISELE

No,—Irene.

IRENE

[*Still off.*] My crêpe de chine gown, Josephine. . . . I'm going to dress right away.

GISELE

But you said you'd wear the white dress!

IRENE

So I did. My white dress, Josephine.

JOSEPHINE

Very good, mademoiselle. [JOSEPHINE *goes to dressing room.*]

GISELE

Irene!

IRENE

You wanted to ask me something?

GISELE

[*Going to door of dressing room and speaking off to* IRENE.] Oh, yes. I overheard something that papa said while I was in my room. Just a few words, but I'm dying to know what they meant.

IRENE

You heard something father said?

GISELE

Yes—not deliberately—I really wasn't listening at the keyhole. But for a moment papa spoke so loudly that I couldn't help hearing.

IRENE

What did you hear?

GISELE

He said, "You'll go or be forced to go!" Surely it wasn't Rome he was speaking about?

IRENE

Yes.

GISELE

What? . . . You're not coming to Rome! . . . Oh, Irene, you can't mean that!

IRENE

I'm not sure yet, dear. Don't bother your head about it.

GISELE

[*Leaving the door, almost in tears*]: You're not going to let me go there alone with papa?

IRENE

[*Enters in negligée*]: I may have to. . . . [*Takes* GISELE's *hand.*]

GISELE

[*Heartbroken*]: Oh!

IRENE

But you'll have a marvelous time in Rome. . . . You've no idea how beautiful it is. You'll meet some delightful people . . . they'll give you any number of parties. Just think, dear, you'll be the only woman in the embassy. . . . You'll have the time of your life!

GISELE

Without you?

IRENE

[*Tenderly*]: Yes, dearest, even without me.

GISELE

How can I—if you're not there?

IRENE

[*Holding her close*]: My dear!

GISELE

Oh, well, if you're going to desert me, then what will—

IRENE

Would you rather stay here with me?

GISELE

Oh, yes—much!

IRENE

But wouldn't you be sorry not to go to Rome?

GISELE

I'd like to have gone if you had gone. But without you—no—I'd much prefer to remain here.

IRENE

Are you sure?

GISELE

Sure.

IRENE

Well, would you like me to persuade father to leave you here too? It won't be easy, but if it's worked well he might consent.

GISELE

Yes, please do.

IRENE

All right, let me try! But you won't say a word to any one, not even to Mademoiselle Marchand, will you?

GISELE

Not a word!

JOSEPHINE

[*Entering left.*] Mademoiselle?

IRENE

Yes, yes.—I'm coming. [*She goes again into the dressing room.* JOSEPHINE *follows her off.*]

GISELE

Oh, Irene! You didn't say a thing about my new frock!

IRENE

[*Off*]: Oh! I'm so sorry! [GISELE *approaches the half-open door.*] I think it's a dream, dear.

GISELE

Don't you think the skirt rather long?

IRENE

[*Still off*]: No. . . . I think it's all right that way.

GISELE

[*Raising her skirt a bit*]: Now—isn't that much better? Look?

IRENE

M-m-m—perhaps. But it was really all right before.

GISELE

Oh! You make me sick! Can't you give a poor woman a little friendly advice?

IRENE

Well . . . no, it *is* a little too short for you. It doesn't look quite modest.

GISELE

Really? But I raised it barely two inches. . . .

IRENE

You've got plenty of time ahead in which to show your legs—

GISELE

Oh, you think so? And what if they begin wearing long skirts again next season, then where am I?

IRENE

There's something in that!

GISELE

Well, suppose I raise it one inch. . . . Are you still horrified?

IRENE

No, go ahead. . . . Shorten it one inch!

GISELE

[*To* JOSEPHINE *who crosses from the dressing room toward the right.*] You heard, Josephine. One inch.

JOSEPHINE

Yes, mademoiselle.

GISELE

I'll pin it up for you in the morning. It can stay like this for to-night. [JOSEPHINE *takes* IRENE'S *coat and hat from chair.*] Who cares about to-night, anyhow?—Whiskers!

IRENE

[*Coming in now fully gowned*]: Josephine!

JOSEPHINE

Yes, mademoiselle?

IRENE

Monsieur Jacques Virieu will be calling to see me. As soon as he arrives, show him in here . . . do you understand?

JOSEPHINE

Yes, mademoiselle. [*Exits at back with coat and hat.* GISELE *has taken from the table the bunch of violets which* IRENE *brought in with her and is absent-mindedly inhaling their odor.*]

GISELE

[*Pleased; turns to* IRENE]: Jacques coming? [IRENE *sees the violets in* GISELE's *hand, a faint movement reveals some indefinable emotion as she takes them from her. She exits into the dressing room returning with the flowers in a vase which she places on the table.* GISELE *watches her, a bit surprised.*] I say, Irene—?

IRENE

What?

GISELE

Is Jacques coming?

IRENE

Yes. . . . I'm expecting him.

GISELE

What fun! . . . Dear old thing! I *will* be glad to see him! But he isn't coming for dinner, is he?

IRENE

No. I asked him to come to see me for a minute because. . . . I've something to tell him. . . . Incidentally, Gisele, be an angel and leave me alone with him after you've said hullo.

GISELE

Righto!

IRENE

Thank you, darling. . . . You're really a dear! You never ask questions . . . and you never ask me to explain a thing!

GISELE

Oh, I just try not to meddle in what isn't my business, that's all.

IRENE

Yes, but they're scarce, people who can do that! [JOSEPHINE *opens the door at back and admits* JACQUES. *He is about thirty-four and good looking.*] Hullo, Jacques! [*Gives him her hand.*]

JACQUES

How are you, Irene? [*To* GISELE]: Well, baby sister!

GISELE

Hullo, Jacques!

JACQUES

Lord, what a beauty! I'm bowled over . . . and to think that I once bounced *this* on my knee! I wouldn't dare try it now!

GISELE

Well, I should hope not! [*The girls laugh.*]

JACQUES

[*Noticing their costumes, to* IRENE]: But, see here, you didn't tell me this was a state occasion!

IRENE

State occasion?

JACQUES

Your gowns. . . !

IRENE

Don't be startled! Father's having some guests to dinner this evening.

JACQUES

Oh, I see. [*Pause.*] Well, what's going on?

GISELE

Before you start in, say good-by to me.

JACQUES

Are you leaving us?

GISELE

I must.

JACQUES

Farewell, beauteous one!

GISELE

When are you having that tea party for Irene and me?

JACQUES

You've only to name your day!

GISELE

The last time I saw you you promised us a sumpt'ous tea with caviar sandwiches. But that's as far as it ever got.

JACQUES

We'll arrange it, I promise!

GISELE

I'm counting on you, don't forget! I just love caviar! [*She goes out at back.*]

JACQUES

Well?

IRENE

Thanks for having come, Jacques.

JACQUES

Please. . . . [*He sits.*] I'm very curious. What's happened?

IRENE

First I want you to swear that you'll never repeat a word of what we're going to say to a living soul. . . .

JACQUES

Is it as serious as that?

IRENE

Yes. . . . You'll swear it, won't you, Jacques?

JACQUES

Why, certainly.

IRENE

You've heard that father has just been appointed to the post in Rome?

JACQUES

Yes.

IRENE

He's decided that Gisele and I are to go there with him.

JACQUES

Naturally.

IRENE

It's not so natural. Until now whenever he occupied a foreign post he's left us here. Why does he want to take us to Rome this time? . . . I can't help thinking he's been advised to do it.

JACQUES

By whom?

IRENE

The Foreign Office probably. It seems they're rather strict in Rome. Perhaps they felt at the Foreign Office that it would look well for him to have his daughters with him . . . and that it would prevent his taking Madame de Vallon as he always has before. I don't think that was liked any too well in Brussels.

JACQUES

Really?

IRENE

I can't be certain that's the reason, but it seems likely. Besides, it doesn't matter. The main point now is that he's decided we're to go with him. [*Pause.*] Only I have decided to remain in Paris.

JACQUES

Why?

IRENE

[*After a moment.*]: . . . I told him it was because of my painting,—so that I might continue to work here with my teacher. . . .

JACQUES

Wasn't that true?

IRENE

No. Besides, to-day, father saw my teacher, who told him I hadn't been at the studio for a month.

JACQUES

I see.

IRENE

He realized I had another reason for staying. We had a very trying scene just now; he wound up by saying that he was sure my desire not to go was due to some one who held me in Paris. He insisted on knowing who it was.

JACQUES

And then?

IRENE

He tormented me with questions which I couldn't answer, threatened to take steps which I couldn't let him take. I was nearly crazy, and then a name came to my lips almost despite myself . . . the name of the only friend I knew I could count on, the only being I could confide in . . . yours.

JACQUES

Mine?

IRENE

Yes.

JACQUES

You gave him my name?

IRENE

Yes.

JACQUES

Then . . . your father believes it's on *my* account that you wish to remain in Paris?

IRENE

Yes.

JACQUES

[*After a moment*]: Do you realize, Irene, what you've done?

IRENE

Yes.

JACQUES

What can your father think?

IRENE

[*Not looking at him*]: Nothing. I told him that by leaving me in Paris—that is, by not taking me away from where you were—a plan which so far I was alone in forming might become a reality. . . .

JACQUES

What plan?

IRENE

That of . . . our getting married.

JACQUES

You led him to believe that?

IRENE

Yes.

JACQUES

No!

IRENE

Yes, I know. . . . I know everything you're thinking.

JACQUES

Wouldn't it have been better to tell him—the truth?

IRENE

[*Sharply, looking at him*]: What truth?

JACQUES

I don't know. But whatever it may be it's certainly better than this—this lie.

IRENE

[*Hopeless. Staring ahead*]: If I had told the truth, no one would have understood it.

JACQUES

Why? [*She is silent.*] Tell me!

IRENE

It doesn't matter. . . .

JACQUES

Can't you at least tell *me?*

IRENE

No.

JACQUES

Ah? [*Pause.*] Well, I confess it's pretty hard for me to understand how you could have disposed of me like this in such a serious situation—without even consulting me!

IRENE

Did I have time to consult you? I was frantic. Every argument I used was turned against me. . . . I saw only one thing—that father had to be reassured about me at any cost . . . so that he'd look no further. That was my one anxiety.

JACQUES

Were you so certain that my name would be enough to reassure him?

IRENE

Yes.

JACQUES

You might have realized, Irene, that you should have used some other name . . . *any* other name. [*He rises impatiently.*]

IRENE

What choice had I? Do you think I have a single friend besides yourself of whom I could ask such a thing?

JACQUES

Didn't it occur to you that perhaps I was the last one of whom you could ask such a thing?

IRENE

I thought you were fond of me.

JACQUES

You didn't remember that I had also loved you?

IRENE

Oh, Jacques . . . that's all in the past.

JACQUES

Are you so sure? [*Pause.*] Certainly it's not so far in the past that you've already forgotten it? Is it?

IRENE

I didn't think about it.

JACQUES

You should have understood that a girl doesn't ask a man to take part in a pretended engagement when he had hoped for the real thing . . . a man, who hardly a year ago had every reason to believe that his hope would be realized!

IRENE

Please, Jacques! Don't remind me of that! I've regretted it so much, believe me! I don't know what could have let you suppose that I'd ever had the idea of—

JACQUES

Of becoming my wife? Then why didn't you stop me right away the first time I told you that I loved you and that I wanted to marry you? . . .

IRENE

But. . . . I didn't think you were really serious about it. . . .

JACQUES

[*With ill-humor*]: Come now! Who jokes about such a thing? Besides if you had thought I was joking you would have replied in the same vein. Instead of that you asked for time to think things over . . . with real sincerity in your voice. [*His manner softens.*] You had to leave for Florence a month later. We saw each other every day before you went. I took you to the station the night you left, and on the platform during the last few minutes before the train pulled out, you said with a smile that I can still see that you were going to send me your answer. [*More coldly.*] Well, I'll never believe that the answer you were planning to send was the one that I finally received three weeks later.

IRENE

You're wrong.

JACQUES

I don't believe it.

IRENE

What—according to you—could have happened to make me change my mind?

JACQUES

I don't know. Something occurred in your life there that I know nothing about, that I haven't tried to find out, but that has changed you in many ways. Of course, it's none of my business . . . but surely I have the right to find it—shall we say unexpected—that you come to me after that, asking me to pose as your fiancé! You must admit it's a bit humorous!

IRENE

I thought you'd have a little more sympathy.

JACQUES

Oh, don't think I'm reproaching you. I just find it humorous, that's all. [*Pause.*] So you told your father that I wanted to marry you and that—

IRENE

I didn't tell him you wanted to marry me. I said merely that *I* wanted to marry . . . but that I was unaware of your intentions.

JACQUES

And your father believed that this desire came to you—like that—with nothing on my part to encourage it? Come, Irene, your father's fully aware of your pride . . . he can't help but think I'm on the verge of telling him I want to marry you.

IRENE

I swear that I've said nothing which might let him suppose so. . . . Anyhow, you'll see that for yourself,—he wants to speak to you.

JACQUES

[*Surprised*]: He wants to speak to me?

IRENE

I did my best to prevent it, but he wouldn't listen. He said he'd see you to-morrow.

JACQUES

Really?

IRENE

You'll see by what he says that I haven't "disposed" of you, as you say. . . . In a moment of distress I turned to you as the one human being who could possibly help me. If you don't want to, there's nothing to compel it. When father questions you, you've only to act as though all this were news to you and surprises you. Say that there's some mistake—that it's a misunderstanding for which you're terribly sorry but which you did nothing to cause and that will be all. You may rest assured that's the last you'll hear of it.

JACQUES

And then,—what will you do?

IRENE

That, Jacques— [*She turns away.*]

JACQUES

Yes. That's none of my business, is that it?

IRENE

What can it matter to you?

JACQUES

[*After a moment*]: But tell me,—before calling

on me to help you, didn't it occur to you that I might not be free, that there might be some one else in my life.

IRENE

I know that there is some one else in your life.

JACQUES

You know it?

IRENE

Yes, of course.

JACQUES

Well, then, since you know it, how could you ask me to do this for you?

IRENE

Am I asking you to change your mode of existence in any way?

JACQUES

Well, what are you asking me? To pose as your fiancé, isn't that it?

IRENE

Not at all! It's simply—

JACQUES

Yes, yes, only so far as your father is concerned.

IRENE

But not even so far as he is concerned. All I ask is that you suggest to him that by taking me away from Paris he might lessen the—the possibility of a marriage between us some day . . . that's all.

JACQUES

In other words, you want to take advantage of the confidence your father has in me to hide something behind it.—I don't know exactly what, but *something*—that you can't confess to any one. It amounts to that, doesn't it?

IRENE

I simply need a few days until father leaves. Afterwards—[*A gesture.*]

JACQUES

What afterwards?

IRENE

Afterwards, I'll manage somehow. [*Determinedly.*] I'll find some way of remaining here. I'll give you back your liberty, I promise you.

JACQUES

But why must you remain here at any cost? Mayn't I know?

IRENE

I don't wish to leave Paris; that's all I can say.

JACQUES

Irene! Let's have the truth. You don't want to leave some one who's in Paris. It's that, isn't it? Eh? [IRENE *is silent. A pause.*] So that's what you've come to. You! . . . You that I admired so much! You whom I've always thought incapable of anything low or cheap. And here you are mixed up in the cheapest of all things—a *lie!*

IRENE

If I lie, it's because I'm driven to it.

JACQUES

By whom?

IRENE

By every one. There's no other course open to me.

JACQUES

That course isn't worth much, believe me. . . . It won't lead you far. And, above all, it's unworthy of you, Irene. You're too fine for that!

IRENE

No, I'm not too fine for that! You've always cherished illusions about me, Jacques. How often

I've asked you not to place me on a pedestal—don't you remember? Why have you always persisted in thinking me different?

JACQUES

Probably because I loved you.

IRENE

Ah! That's not my fault.

JACQUES

And then, *no*, it's not true! . . . You were different! Only you've changed . . . or rather they've changed you—

IRENE

[*Aggressively.*] They? Who?

JACQUES

No doubt the people you've been with such a lot this past year. In deserting your old friends for them it doesn't seem to me that you have profited by the change.

IRENE

These "people" as you call them . . . do you know them?

JACQUES

Not at all.

IRENE

Well, then— [*Pause.*] Think what you wish of them but don't tell me about it, do you mind?

JACQUES

[*Angrily*]: Very well! But since they mean so much to you why didn't you turn to one of them for the help you need? It seems to me that would be far more natural. Especially, as I'm not exactly the man for this sort of game.

IRENE

[*Beseeching*]: Jacques!

JACQUES

You must have some real friends among them—one surely—well, ask him.

IRENE

I have only one real friend—you. . . . At least I thought you were my friend.

JACQUES

It's just because I am your friend that I haven't the right to do what you ask.

IRENE

Why?

JACQUES

Because it's unpleasant, dangerous—and, above all, useless. No good can come of a lie like that. It's doomed in advance.

IRENE

If you were really my friend, you'd let yourself be guided by your heart . . . instead of by the rules of middle class morality.

JACQUES

Middle class morality has its good points.

IRENE

[*Ironically*]: Yes . . . especially to those who profit by it!

JACQUES

What does that mean?

IRENE

Were you being prompted by the rules of that morality last year when you asked me to be your mistress? You remember that . . . ?

JACQUES

Yes, I do.

IRENE

Highly moral, that?

JACQUES

Yes.

IRENE

Ah!

JACQUES

Yes, because if you had belonged to me, you'd have ended by loving me and marrying me. I'd have overcome your unwillingness to give up your liberty. . . . It would have been a step toward the only solution of any girl's life—marriage.

IRENE

Then it was to convert me to marriage that you wanted me to give myself to you?

JACQUES

Yes.

IRENE

Really? [*Pause.*] I had thought it was merely because you wanted me.

JACQUES

Naturally I wanted you. I wanted you with all my heart. The thought of your body against mine stirred my blood—as it does at this minute, if you must know!

IRENE

Jacques!

JACQUES

I'm beginning to think I'll never get over my love for you. However, that's neither here nor there, and doesn't interest you. . . . What I want to tell you is that it's always you of whom I think . . . even before myself, do you hear? Even now. So that you won't doubt it, I'll say this:—swear to me that this affair of yours—about which I don't ask to know anything—will eventually lead to a marriage worthy of you . . . just swear that and I'll do anything you want me to do. Can you swear it?

IRENE

[*Turning away*]: . . . I won't swear to anything.

JACQUES

Very well. Then, I refuse. Think what you like . . . that I'm heartless, that I don't love you—I don't care. I refuse. And if my refusal makes you give up this affair a bit sooner than you expected, it will be better all around, you may be sure.

IRENE

[*With intense feeling*]: You ought to know me well enough, Jacques, to realize that I'll do what

I've decided to do . . . even if doing so shatters everything.

JACQUES

Have you gone crazy?

IRENE

[*Wildly*]: No! But I will if I'm forced to leave. . . .

JACQUES

Irene! [IRENE *lowers her head, repressing her emotion.* GISELE *enters, at back.*]

GISELE

Jacques, papa says not to go,—he wants to speak to you.

IRENE

[*Alarmed*]: How did he know Jacques was here?

GISELE

Why, I told him. He just got back. He took one look at the table and said it looked like nothing at all! So he told me to fetch you and I said you were with Jacques. [*Pause. Penitently to* IRENE.] Shouldn't I have said that?

IRENE

[*Embarrassed*]: That's all right, dear.

GISELE

So he sent me to ask Jacques to wait because he wanted to see him, that's all. . . . [*To* JACQUES.] Did I put my foot in it . . . ?

JACQUES

No, Gisele, it doesn't matter.

GISELE

Well, I couldn't know! You should have warned me. [*She goes out.* JACQUES *closes door.*]

[IRENE *stands rigid for a moment, then suddenly making up her mind, hurries into the dressing room emerging with a cloak which she throws about her as she heads for the door, back.*]

JACQUES

[*Barring the way*]: What are you doing? . . . You're going out?

IRENE

I'm leaving here.

JACQUES

Where are you going?

IRENE

[*Hotly*]: That's my business. . . . I'm going, that's all.

JACQUES

But, Irene—

IRENE

Let me go!

JACQUES

Why do you want to leave?

IRENE

It'll put an end to all this!

JACQUES

You're not in your right senses now!

IRENE

Let me pass!

JACQUES

What shall I say to your father?

IRENE

Whatever you like, I don't care. . . . Let me pass!

JACQUES

No!

IRENE

You've no right to stop me from doing what I want.

JACQUES

I've a right to stop your doing something rash!

IRENE

[*In a torment of terror and despair*]: I've had enough! Enough! I'm twenty-five, free to do as I like without accounting to any one. Let me pass! Jacques!

JACQUES

Irene, come, calm yourself, I beg of you!

IRENE

Do you realize what my life here will be after father has spoken to you? No! No! I'll not be questioned any more! I can't stand this being baited by the world! I want to go away!

JACQUES

Irene!

IRENE

After all, what difference does it make to you if I go?

JACQUES

What difference does it make to me?

IRENE

[*In cold fury*]: Yes,—is it any business of yours?

JACQUES

[*After a pause, leaving her*]: You're quite right. Very well, go. [*He comes forward and sits near the table, his head in his hands.* IRENE, *without moving, follows him with her eyes.*] Well, why don't you go? What's keeping you from going to him, now? [*A wan smile crosses* IRENE'S *face. She wraps her cloak around her and goes slowly to the door, which she is about to open. He sits up.*] Irene!

IRENE

[*Turning back*]: Yes?

JACQUES

[*After a pause; curtly*]: Stay here!

IRENE

What?

JACQUES

Stay here, I say.

IRENE

I don't understand.

JACQUES

Yes you do, you understand perfectly. . . . Take

off your wrap. If your father sees it, he's the one who won't understand.

IRENE

But explain what you—

JACQUES

Do as I say. [MONTCEL *enters at back.* IRENE, *hidden by the door, lets her cloak slip off.* MONTCEL *crosses to* JACQUES.]

MONTCEL

Good evening, Jacques.

JACQUES

Good evening, uncle.

MONTCEL

I hope you didn't mind waiting.

JACQUES

Not at all.

MONTCEL

I was going to drop you a line asking you to come in to see me to-morrow, but when I heard you were here with Irene I thought I'd save you the trouble. . . . I wanted to have a chat with you. Shall we go along to my study? [JACQUES *assents.*] I won't keep you long. [*Takes* JACQUES *to door—sees* IRENE—*stops.*] Go ahead, I'll join you. [JACQUES *goes out.* MONTCEL *quickly to* IRENE.] You've already spoken to him, haven't you?

IRENE

What do you mean?

MONTCEL

Well, if he knows—tell me. It will save a lot of useless talk.

IRENE

[*After a moment.*] Yes.

MONTCEL

Well? . . . What's his answer?

IRENE

He'll tell you himself.

MONTCEL

Good. [*He goes out.* IRENE *remains there, thoughtful, brooding, her face woeful. After a moment, her eyes light on the vase which contains the violets; she is drawn over to them, looks at them, touches them delicately. Then, as if an idea had taken her, she regards her watch, half hesitates and reaches for the telephone. She lifts the receiver with intense anticipation as*

THE CURTAIN FALLS

THE CAPTIVE

ACT TWO

SCENE: *A study in* JACQUES' *apartment. It has a bookish, comfortable appearance. There are doors at back to the hall, at right to a bedroom and at left to a small salon or reception room. A large desk stands center. A few good-sized chairs and a massive leather divan are placed about.*

It is a month later.

At the rise JACQUES *is discovered seated, musing deeply, his eyes staring ahead. On his lap he has an open snapshot album neglected for the moment.*

A door bell sounds, JACQUES *scowls, regards his watch and, rising, murmurs,* "Oh, well!"

GEORGES, *his man, enters.*

GEORGES

Are you at home, monsieur?

JACQUES

I'm expecting Madame Meillant. It's probably she.

GEORGES

Yes, monsieur. [*He goes out.* JACQUES *places the album in a drawer of desk.* GEORGES *returns.*] It's not Madame Meillant, monsieur; it's Mademoiselle de Montcel.

JACQUES

[*Surprised*]: Mademoiselle de Montcel?

GEORGES

Yes, monsieur.

JACQUES

[*Nervously*]: Have you shown her into the salon?

GEORGES

Yes, monsieur.

JACQUES

Very well. [*He goes toward door which leads to the salon.*] Oh! When Madame Meillant comes tell her—tell her that I telephoned I'd be a bit late. Say that I hope she'll forgive me and ask if she'd mind coming back at four, if that's convenient. [*Looks at his watch.*] That's it, at four.

GEORGES

Very good, monsieur. [*He goes out.* JACQUES *opens door to salon.*]

JACQUES

Do come in— [*Surprised.*] Why, it's—? Well! My man said it was Mademoiselle de Montcel so I thought—

GISELE

[*Entering*]: That it was Irene?

JACQUES

Yes.

GISELE

Oh, I'm so sorry, Jacques.

JACQUES

But not at all—why?

GISELE

Because you must be terribly disappointed!

JACQUES

Not at all, my dear. [*Closes door.*] I'm delighted to see you. A bit surprised, but delighted.

GISELE

You're surprised because you think that a girl of my age shouldn't come alone to a man's apartment, is that it? But I didn't come alone. Mademoiselle Marchand is waiting downstairs in the car.

JACQUES

You've no need to explain. Do sit down!

GISELE

I've just one thing to tell you.

JACQUES

Sit down anyway.

GISELE

[*Sits*]: At first I thought I'd telephone you this morning to ask when I could come, but the phone's in Irene's room and I didn't want her to hear.

JACQUES

I see.

GISELE

So instead I came early to have a better chance of finding you in. . . . [*She hesitates.*] Jacques, perhaps you're going to think that what I'm doing is a bit ridiculous and even uncalled for—but I don't care. It's just this—I've come to tell you that Irene is very unhappy.

JACQUES

Irene?

GISELE

Yes . . . and you can believe me. . . . I'm saying this only because I'm sure of it. For some time now she's been acting in a very strange, nervous way. Several times it seemed to me that her eyes were rather red. Mademoiselle Marchand had also noticed it. And the other day I went into her room to phone, thinking she'd gone out, and, although she turned her face away, I saw she was crying.

JACQUES

Ah?

GISELE

For Irene to cry means that something's really wrong. I can't bear seeing her wretched! Anything rather than that. I thought it over and decided you didn't know about it and that you should. That's why I've come. So, Jacques—that's all. [*A pause.*] Are you annoyed with me for telling you this?

JACQUES

I'm not annoyed with you at all, my dear,—only I must confess that I don't quite understand why you thought you ought to tell *me* about it!

GISELE

What?

JACQUES

I'm very fond of Irene but I don't see that I—

GISELE

[*Smiling*]: Jacques . . . papa told me before he left.

JACQUES

[*Surprised and rather annoyed*]: What did he tell you?

GISELE

Oh, don't worry! He swore me to secrecy—and you may be sure I'll never tell a soul. Besides, I realize that you both want to think things over, and that you don't feel free to commit yourself definitely just now because of your business troubles. . . . I know all that. . . . [JACQUES *is disturbed and wretched.*] . . . Are you cross that papa told me?

JACQUES

No, no, it doesn't matter.

GISELE

You see, it would have been difficult for him *not* to say something. It had been all arranged that we were to go to Rome with him. Then suddenly plans are changed; we're to remain here—with Mademoiselle Marchand living at the house as chaperon. So papa probably felt obliged to give me *some* explanation. He didn't realize that I had already guessed everything.

JACQUES

What—what had you guessed?

GISELE

Everything! After all, it wasn't so brilliant of me! I knew that Irene wanted to stay in Paris and that papa wouldn't hear of it. Then on top of that, you come to see Irene, you have a talk with papa, and the same evening he announces to Irene that she may remain and that he'll leave me with her. Well, I didn't have to be so awfully bright to understand what all that meant. [*Rises.*] And, Jacques, I was so happy when I *did* understand. I can't begin to tell you how happy!

JACQUES

Really?

GISELE

I'm positive you're just made for one another! Don't you think so too?

JACQUES

Of course, my dear.

GISELE

So now you understand why I came?

JACQUES

I understand.

GISELE

Was it wrong of me to come?

JACQUES

No.

GISELE

And it's true that you had noticed nothing, isn't it?

JACQUES

Nothing.

GISELE

I was sure of it! I said to Mademoiselle Marchand: "If Jacques asked papa to leave Irene in Paris, it's because he loves her, and if he loves her he can't want her to be miserable . . . or else he hasn't noticed it. And, naturally, if no one does anything it all might go on forever! And it must not go on." [*She takes his hand.*] Must it, Jacques?

JACQUES

No, it mustn't, Gisele dear. Only, don't you see—

GISELE

No, don't tell me. I don't want to know anything. It's none of my business. I've told you what I wanted to say. The rest is your affair. I ask just one thing—never let Irene know I came here, because she'd never forgive me for it. Promise?

Photograph by Florence Vandamm

IRENE: It's like—a prison to which I must return captive, despite myself.
(HELEN MENKEN *and* BASIL RATHBONE)

JACQUES

I promise.

GISELE

Thank you. [*She lets go his hand.*]

JACQUES

Wait, please don't go yet, do you mind? [*He walks about, thinking, then stops in front of her.*] Do you trust me, Gisele?

GISELE

[*Surprised and a bit worried*]: Why, Jacques, of course!

JACQUES

Enough to believe me without asking for explanations?

GISELE

[*Still anxious*]: Yes, what is it?

JACQUES

You think—and it's natural enough you should—that I could prevent Irene's being unhappy if I wanted to, don't you?

GISELE

Yes.

JACQUES

Well, you're mistaken.

GISELE

What?

JACQUES

I can do nothing for her . . . or so little. . . .

GISELE

You?

JACQUES

I.

GISELE

Then it's not because of you that she's unhappy?

JACQUES

No.

GISELE

[*Astonished*]: No? . . .

JACQUES

If it were because of me, believe me she'd not be unhappy long. Of course I can try to do something for her. It may accomplish nothing, but I can try. Only for that I'll need you.

GISELE

Me?

JACQUES

Yes. I need some information that only you can give me. If I knew of any one else to turn to, I would, but, if you think my questions are indiscreet or if you believe they are prompted by anything but my desire to see Irene happy, don't answer them.

GISELE

What do you want to know?

JACQUES

I'd like to know something about the life she leads, the people she sees.

GISELE

The people she sees? Why *you*, mostly.

JACQUES

Me?

GISELE

Yes.

JACQUES

When does she see me?

GISELE

Well—I don't know. Don't you always have tea together?

JACQUES

Did she tell you that?

GISELE

[*Puzzled*]: I had understood that. . . . I might have been mistaken.

JACQUES

[*After a pause*]: And besides myself, whom does she see?

GISELE

Well, you know, she doesn't tell me a great deal about what she does.

JACQUES

When she goes out, doesn't she ever tell you where she is going?

GISELE

She goes to the studio every day after lunch.

JACQUES

Ah, yes. . . . And at night, does she ever go out?

GISELE

At night? Oh, almost never. She's been once or twice to the theater or a concert, but that's all.

JACQUES

Alone?

GISELE

No, with Monsieur and Madame d'Aiguines.

JACQUES

Oh. [*After a pause.*] She met them in Italy, didn't she?

GISELE

Yes, in Florence, last year.

JACQUES

Do you ever see them?

GISELE

I? Never!

JACQUES

Why?

GISELE

I don't know them.

JACQUES

How is it you've never met them if Irene is so intimate with them?

GISELE

That's no reason. She never suggested my meeting them and I never asked to.

JACQUES

Why? Don't you like them?

GISELE

But I don't know them.

JACQUES

Does she ever speak to you about them?

GISELE

No, never.

JACQUES

And have you never had curiosity enough to ask her questions about them?

GISELE

I never ask Irene questions. When she speaks to me first about some one or something—well and good. But when she doesn't, she doesn't, that's all.

JACQUES

So, you know nothing about the d'Aiguines?

GISELE

Very little. I know that *she* is Polish or Austrian, I don't remember which.

JACQUES

But you know nothing about him?

GISELE

Nothing.

JACQUES

You don't know what he does, whether he has any business?

GISELE

I've no idea.

JACQUES

You don't know either—what he's like?

GISELE

Oh, his looks?

JACQUES

Yes.

GISELE

He's tall, clean shaven—rather smart.

JACQUES

Then you've seen him?

GISELE

Yes.

JACQUES

Where have you seen him?

GISELE

At the front door one evening when he had brought Irene home. I happened to be going in at the same time and saw him. Why?

JACQUES

I went to school with a chap by the name of d'Aiguines. I was wondering if it were the same.

GISELE

Oh, I don't think so. He's quite a bit older than you.

JACQUES

Ah? . . . Perhaps he's a cousin, then. . . . There are several branches of the family. . . . [*Pause.*] Is that the only time you've ever met him?

GISELE

Yes. I heard his voice on the telephone one day when he called up and Irene was out. That's all.

JACQUES

Does he ever come to see her?

GISELE

At home? No, never—

JACQUES

Do you know where they live?

GISELE

Avenue Victor Hugo, but I've forgotten the number. They're in the telephone book.

JACQUES

[*Thoughtful*]: Good.

GISELE

The d'Aiguines interest you as much as that?

JACQUES

Oh! They interest me—because they're friends of Irene, that's all.

GISELE

Is that all you wanted to ask me?

JACQUES

Yes, my dear, thank you. You haven't told me much I didn't already know, as a matter of fact. But our talk hasn't been without value. [*Pause.*] Oh!—it's understood that Irene must never know about it.

GISELE

I promise you that.

JACQUES

I know I can trust you.

GISELE

[*Hesitatingly*]: Jacques, before I go—I *should* like to—to ask you a question.

JACQUES

Why, certainly.

GISELE

Can't you tell me what you're going to do to help Irene?

JACQUES

No, Gisele. Besides my plan has such slight chance of success. . . .

GISELE

Yes, but you wouldn't attempt it, would you, if you didn't think it might succeed?

JACQUES

Well, let's say the chances are about one in ten.

GISELE

Well, if it does succeed would it—would it mean that you'd get married? Tell me?

JACQUES

No.

GISELE

Ah! [*Pause.*] And yet you love her?

JACQUES

[*Smiling wanly*]: Do you believe so?

GISELE

Oh, come! I've known it for ever so long. You've been in love with her ever since the summer you spent at Montcel.

JACQUES

But that's not enough, you see.

GISELE

You mean that she doesn't love you?

JACQUES

Yes, just that.

GISELE

Are you sure?

JACQUES

Absolutely.

GISELE

What a pity! . . . [*She hesitates; then realizes there is no more to be said.*] Good-by, Jacques.

JACQUES

Good-by, dear child.

[*She looks at him sadly, takes his hand, then with a sudden, tender movement, kisses him on both cheeks and exits. He goes with her, enters again a few seconds later, sits at his desk and ponders. Picks up telephone book, looks up a number, then calls.*]

Passy 83-42. . . . Hello, is this Monsieur d'Aiguines' house? . . . Is Monsieur d'Aiguines at home? . . . Oh! . . . well, can you give me his office address? Where? . . . [*He writes on pad.*] Thank you very much. Do you happen to know until what time he'll be there? . . . Thank you.

[*Hangs up receiver, takes writing-paper and begins to write. After writing a few lines, re-reads what he's written, appears irritated, crumples it up and takes a fresh sheet. When he has fin-*

ished, he rings, puts letter in envelope, addresses it. GEORGES *enters.*]

GEORGES

Did you ring, monsieur?

JACQUES

Yes. Jump into a taxi and take this letter to this address. It's a bank. If they tell you that the gentleman is in, deliver the letter and wait for an answer. [*A door bell is heard.*] If he's not in, bring me back the letter and ask if there is a chance of finding him there to-morrow morning. You needn't leave my name—it's not necessary.

GEORGES

Yes, monsieur.

JACQUES

You quite understand?

GEORGES

Yes, monsieur.

JACQUES

See who is at the door.

GEORGES

[*Going toward door, back*]: If it is Madame Meillant, monsieur, what shall I say? [*Bell rings again with insistence.*]

JACQUES

[*Smiling*]: It *is* Madame Meillant—show her in.

[GEORGES *goes out, enters a moment later with* FRANÇOISE, *an exceedingly handsome young woman, smartly attired.* GEORGES *leaves.*]

FRANÇOISE

Well, I thought you were going to leave me planted on the doorstep. You must tell Georges to open the door more quickly. One always runs into some one on stairways. [*She moves about, very much at home.*]

JACQUES

I love your plural! [*Lights cigarette at desk.*]

FRANÇOISE

What?

JACQUES

Nothing. It's not Georges' fault, it's mine. I was giving him an order.

FRANÇOISE

Huh, that only makes it worse! [*After pause, turns to him.*] Hullo, dear!

JACQUES

Hullo, Françoise.

FRANÇOISE

Well! After all . . . !

JACQUES

But you don't give me a chance to open my mouth. [*He gives her a light kiss.*]

FRANÇOISE

You're not in a very pleasant mood to-day.

JACQUES

I? Of course, I am.

FRANÇOISE

Why didn't you come to the Van Gartens' last night?

JACQUES

I couldn't get there.

FRANÇOISE

I waited until twelve-thirty for you to come, and I had a beastly headache. At least you might have let me know.

JACQUES

But I told you it wasn't likely I'd be there.

FRANÇOISE

I know. But I'd begged you so hard to at least

try to call for me, that I thought surely you'd make a special effort. Apparently the day is past for me to ask that sort of thing.

JACQUES

I'm so sorry, Françoise.

FRANÇOISE

What were you doing that was so entertaining—if I'm not being indiscreet?

JACQUES

I was dining at my brother's house and it was very late when I left.

FRANÇOISE

Couldn't you have told him you were due at a party?

JACQUES

He'd just come back to town. I hadn't seen him for two months.

FRANÇOISE

Evidently that was more amusing than coming to fetch me.

JACQUES

Well, yes. Frankly, you know I hate those parties—

FRANÇOISE

You hate everything I like.

JACQUES

No, I don't, my dear.

FRANÇOISE

You do. It's always like that—I'm beginning to get used to it. [*Pause.*] Only it's possible you made a mistake by not coming last night—

JACQUES

[*His thoughts elsewhere*]: Really?

FRANÇOISE

Oh, I say that, but really everything's of so little interest to you now—

JACQUES

What's of so little interest to me?

FRANÇOISE

Well, for instance, that some one should have paid me—very marked attention.

JACQUES

Some one paid you very marked attention?

FRANÇOISE

Yes— [*Pause.*] Oh, you know well enough that when a woman has been seen frequently with the same man, and then suddenly is noticed arriving and leaving alone, other men begin to take new interest in her. Besides, last night, I had on a very becoming gown—

JACQUES

Which one?

FRANÇOISE

You haven't seen it. I had hesitated before ordering it because of you—imagine that!—I thought you might find it rather *décolleté*. But I'm glad I took it now. It was a terrific success!

JACQUES

I'm so glad, darling!

FRANÇOISE

I knew it was a sensation as soon as I arrived—from the way the women looked at it!

JACQUES

Not by the way the men looked at it?

FRANÇOISE

Yes, but a bit later. Women notice that sort of thing more quickly.

JACQUES

Ah?

FRANÇOISE

Then, too, I think that I was in great form last night.

JACQUES

In spite of the headache?

FRANÇOISE

In spite of the headache. At least I was told so any number of times.

JACQUES

By whom, for instance?

FRANÇOISE

What do you care?

JACQUES

I'm very interested. You don't doubt that, I hope?

FRANÇOISE

Well, let me see. . . . Several of the men who were there . . . your friend Moreuil, by the way, didn't leave my side all evening.

JACQUES

Oh! I thought he was in America?

FRANÇOISE

He's come back—come back, what's more, an amorous devil. He insisted on seeing me to my door, and he was about to suggest coming up with me.

JACQUES

Not really?

FRANÇOISE

I think in fact—between ourselves—that he *did* suggest it.

JACQUES

[*Smiling indifferently*]: Good old Moreuil. [*Puts out cigarette.* FRANÇOISE *is piqued and gives him a glowering look.*] And so, you were saying that he—

FRANÇOISE

[*Rises impatiently*]: Oh! Please! That's enough, isn't it? Let's speak about something else!

JACQUES

As you say.

FRANÇOISE

Listen, Jacques. When I came I'd no idea of making a scene. But it really begins to look as if you were trying to exasperate me! I've stood for a great deal for some time, but this is too much!

JACQUES

All right, let's have it!

FRANÇOISE

I understand well enough that you don't love me any more; that's quite within your rights. But that being the case, why not say it? We've never sworn eternal fidelity, have we? Be frank about it for once—it would be so much better.

JACQUES

But nothing is changed, Françoise.

FRANÇOISE

Ah, you think not, do you? . . . Well, let me tell you that if you had never shown more ardor than you have to-day I never would have been to you what I have. Ah! . . . No! . . . I realize now that I gave in much too soon. You'd have loved me more if I had made you want me longer. I liked you and let you see that I did; so much the worse for me. At least in the beginning I could entertain some illusions about our love! But *now*—!

JACQUES

I give you my word, Françoise, that my feeling for you has not changed in the least.

FRANÇOISE

What does that mean?

JACQUES

Well, that—

FRANÇOISE

That you have never loved me, is that it?

JACQUES

I didn't say that.

FRANÇOISE

But it's what you're thinking. Well, at least you're being frank about it, thank heaven! At last! But if you never loved me why did you ask me to become—to become your—

JACQUES

[*Breaking in quietly*]: I might reply that I never asked you to.

FRANÇOISE

You never asked me?

JACQUES

No, Françoise.

FRANÇOISE

So! Well, then I—

JACQUES

But don't you remember—

FRANÇOISE

Then I suppose it was I who begged you to become my lover?

JACQUES

No—

FRANÇOISE

Well one of us must have done it—if not you—then it must be I!

JACQUES

Listen, Françoise, let's speak about something else.

FRANÇOISE

No! Not until you've explained what you meant.

JACQUES

Let's pretend that I didn't say anything.

FRANÇOISE

No, no, no! You can't get out of it like that. It would be too easy to insult a person, and then—

JACQUES

How have I insulted you?

FRANÇOISE

Well, if you don't think it insulting to tell a woman who has been your mistress for six months that you never asked her to be, then just what is it?

JACQUES

In that case I offer all kinds of apologies. I simply yielded for the moment to the desire of relating what happened between us. I was wrong. Do forgive me.

FRANÇOISE

Relating what happened between us? You're going back to that?

JACQUES

My dear, try to recall the first talk we had!

FRANÇOISE

Our first talk?

JACQUES

One of the first, if you prefer. It was at Versailles, by the lake. You had telephoned me in the morning to ask if I cared to motor out into the country. We left your car at the entrance of the grounds—if you remember—

FRANÇOISE

I remember, yes.

JACQUES

And you said: "The biggest mistake that women make is to select the same man to make love and to talk about it." I thought that was an amusing idea and I replied, "One can hardly expect to be at the head of one's class in both rhetoric and gymnastics!" You agreed with me and were charming enough to add that I must be at the foot of my class in rhetoric! Finally, you said you saw no reason why two people who were physically attracted to each other should not establish an intimacy,—it being thoroughly understood that there would be no trespassing on the domain of sentiment. The idea delighted me, and as it was time for tea I suggested that we return to town and have it at my apartment . . . which you were good enough to accept. . . . That is exactly how it all happened.

FRANÇOISE

And what has that to do with it?

JACQUES

I always thought that that day we settled the exact relation between us.

FRANÇOISE

[*Shrugging her shoulders*]: As if one meant seriously everything said at such times.

JACQUES

I meant what I said. I only undertook a relation I could abide by. If I had undertaken any other it would have been very unfair to you.

FRANÇOISE

You're being that now, my dear. Do you think that falling in love with me was beneath you?

JACQUES

It's not a question of that!

FRANÇOISE

Strange as it may seem to you, there are many men who feel differently about it.

JACQUES

But I'm aware of that, Françoise! You're a very attractive woman and I know perfectly that there are many men who would like to be in my place. I'm sorry I can't make myself more clear. I only meant to say that at the time of our meeting, I could make no other promises—than those I made—that's all.

FRANÇOISE

Because you were in love with some one else, no doubt. . . . And you still love her, is that it? Say it! Why don't you say it?

JACQUES

That, Françoise, belongs in the domain of sentiment. I have never trespassed on yours, you must admit. Keep off mine.

FRANÇOISE

Do I know her?

JACQUES

Please.

FRANÇOISE

You won't tell me?

JACQUES

There's nothing to tell.

FRANÇOISE

Oh! I'll find out . . . it can't be very difficult. . . . Who is she?

JACQUES

I assure you, Françoise, that you're wasting your time.

FRANÇOISE

[*Searching*]: Let's see; a woman that you were already in love with six months ago and who does not love you—

JACQUES

How do you know that she doesn't love me?

FRANÇOISE

That's evident. Else why should you have turned elsewhere for distraction. That's really all I've been to you—a distraction!

JACQUES

You're mistaken, Françoise.

FRANÇOISE

You're very kind, but don't bother to protest further. . . . I know who she is.

JACQUES

Ah?

FRANCOISE

The Barentier girl?

JACQUES

Now you have it!

FRANÇOISE

It's not she!

JACQUES

Yes, yes, let's say it is!

FRANÇOISE

Great heavens! You're annoying!

JACQUES

Françoise, please, let's change the subject. [GEORGES *enters*]: Pardon me. . . . [*To* GEORGES.] Well?

GEORGES

I delivered the letter.

JACQUES

Did you see the gentleman?

GEORGES

Yes, monsieur. He didn't write an answer but he asked to say that he was coming here to see you.

JACQUES

Really? When?

GEORGES

Now, monsieur.

JACQUES

What, you mean right away?

GEORGES

Yes, monsieur. He asked if you were at home. I said I thought you were. Then he said he was coming.

JACQUES

[*After a pause*]: All right. . . . When he rings, ask him to go into the salon.

GEORGES

Yes, monsieur. [*Exits.*]

FRANÇOISE

Are you expecting some one?

JACQUES

Yes. I hope you'll forgive me, Françoise. It's a man whom I must see about a business matter—a rather important one—concerning my interests in Morocco.

FRANÇOISE

Why, yes, of course.

JACQUES

I wasn't expecting him. Not to-day at least, otherwise—

FRANÇOISE

It doesn't matter at all. [*Goes to divan, gets hat and things.*] As a matter of fact, there was very little left for us to say to each other—wasn't there? [*Pulls hat on.*]

JACQUES

But—I don't know, Françoise.

FRANÇOISE

You see, Jacques, I've only just realized that for the past six months it's I who have given a bit too much both the questions and the answers. So now, I think there's been enough of it and the best thing we can do is put a period at the end of our page. [*He helps her on with her coat.*] Don't you think so too?

JACQUES

Just as you please.

FRANÇOISE

Ah! Well—

JACQUES

What?

FRANÇOISE

Oh, nothing: I feared you might have made some protest—merely as a matter of form. But I see that you've bravely made up your mind—and don't even regard it worth while to protest. Splendid! Let me congratulate you on your resignation— [*Pause.*] What are you thinking?

JACQUES

[*Whose mind is on other things*]: Why—of you and what you've just said. . . .

FRANÇOISE

No, you weren't.

JACQUES

I'm sorry, Françoise. As a matter of fact I was worrying a bit about this coming interview. Do forgive me. Can't we meet again some time soon—perhaps to-morrow?

FRANÇOISE

What for?

JACQUES

I'd like to explain—to attempt to make my position clear.

FRANÇOISE

I assure you, my dear, that I've understood you perfectly!

[*She cries a little but controls herself quickly.*]

JACQUES

[*Going toward her*]: Françoise—

FRANÇOISE

Pay no attention to me!— There, it's over. And now let's say good-by to each other sweetly like the two good friends that we are. I shall miss you, Jacques, dear!

JACQUES

Come, Françoise—

FRANÇOISE

Yes, I will. Oh, it's not your fault—you're the sort of man one misses. After all, we have some rather pleasant memories to look back upon, haven't we?

JACQUES

Yes, dear . . . delightful memories.

FRANÇOISE

You see, Jacques, when a woman promises to love you, you mustn't always believe her. But when a woman promises not to, well, then you mustn't believe her either.

JACQUES

My dear Françoise! . . .

FRANÇOISE

Come, we mustn't weaken now!

JACQUES

But at least, you'll let me write, won't you?

FRANÇOISE

Do! Write me a letter filled with sweetly melancholy thoughts on the way all things come to an end, and send it by the florist with a few of those lovely carnations that I like. I'll wait until they're quite faded before trying to put you out of my thoughts. Good-by.

[*She gives him her hand. He kisses it. The bell is heard. He drops her hand and goes up to the door. She follows.*]

JACQUES

Wait a moment, won't you?

[GEORGES *enters. To* GEORGES.] Is it the gentleman?

GEORGES

Yes, monsieur.

JACQUES

Very well.

FRANÇOISE

[*Moved*]: Don't forget the carnations. [*He goes out with her. In a moment he reënters and goes to the door of the salon and opens it.*]

JACQUES

[*Talking off*]: Would you mind coming in here, monsieur?

[JACQUES *moves a little away from door.* D'AIGUINES *enters past him and turns to* JACQUES *with outstretched hand.*]

D'AIGUINES

How are you, old boy?

JACQUES

Why, it's—

D'AIGUINES

Of course it is! Didn't you know you were writing to me?

JACQUES

Why, no, otherwise—

D'AIGUINES

Otherwise you wouldn't have been so formal, I hope. But didn't my name mean anything to you?

JACQUES

Of course. But I was led to believe that the d'Aiguines I had to deal with was somewhat older.

D'AIGUINES

Somewhat older? Why?

JACQUES

Well, it doesn't matter. I remember you had some cousins. I thought perhaps it might be one of them.

D'AIGUINES

Ah? . . . But what's the reason for—

JACQUES

I'll tell you. [*Pause.*] Do sit down!

D'AIGUINES

[*Puts hat and gloves on desk*]: You're looking at me? . . . You find I've changed, eh? . . . I'm sure you'd hardly have recognized me?

JACQUES

Yes. . . . I would have.

D'AIGUINES

Good Lord, it's something like twenty years since we've seen each other. Not since the days when we wore our trousers out sitting on the same bench at school. Twenty years leave their mark! On some people at least. . . . But you've hardly changed. I'm very glad to see you again, old chap.

JACQUES

Thanks.

D'AIGUINES

It's strange we shouldn't have met. Of course I haven't been in France much. What have you been doing? Weren't you in Morocco for a time?

JACQUES

Yes.

D'AIGUINES

Who was it told me so? [*A pause.*] . . . Ah, yes, I remember; it was Sicard—you remember him —fat Sicard? I met him one day in Madrid. We were staying at the same hotel. He had just returned from Africa, I think, and had seen you there.

JACQUES

Yes.

D'AIGUINES

And now you're living here altogether?

JACQUES

Yes.

D'AIGUINES

Damn funny thing, life. You really didn't know that the d'Aiguines you were writing to for an appointment was I?

JACQUES

No.

D'AIGUINES

Well, the minute I saw your signature I didn't hesitate. That's why I came here right away. If Jacques Virieu wanted to see me I certainly couldn't keep him waiting!

JACQUES

[*Pause*]: Is that the only reason you came here right away?

D'AIGUINES

[*Surprised*]: Good Lord! Since I haven't the least idea what you have to say to me—

JACQUES

You haven't the least idea?

D'AIGUINES

Why, of course not—no.

JACQUES

Ah . . . ?

D'AIGUINES

Well, look here, you arouse my curiosity! Upon my word, you sit there looking like a judge! Come, what's it all about?

JACQUES

Whom is it all about, might me better.

D'AIGUINES

Whom? . . . All right, if you prefer it. Well, then, whom is it all about?

JACQUES

[*Pause*]: About Irene de Montcel.

D'AIGUINES

[*Amazed and annoyed*]: Irene de Montcel?

JACQUES

Yes. [*Pause.*] You seem to begin to understand!

D'AIGUINES

No. What can you have to say to me about Mademoiselle de Montcel?

JACQUES

You can't guess?

D'AIGUINES

No, I can't!

JACQUES

I'm a distant cousin of hers. But what's more important is that I've been a friend of hers for a long time. One of her best friends—I might even say her best friend, if you wish.

D'AIGUINES

Well?

JACQUES

You knew that, didn't you?

D'AIGUINES

I didn't even know you were acquainted.

JACQUES

Have you never heard her speak of me?

D'AIGUINES

Never.

JACQUES

She hasn't even spoken of the—rôle that some one was playing for her at the present time?

D'AIGUINES

What rôle?

JACQUES

Don't you know that some one is pretending to Irene's father to be engaged to her, or something of the sort?

D'AIGUINES

Engaged to her?

JACQUES

To ward off her father's suspicions; and to permit her to remain in Paris, yes.

D'AIGUINES

[*Pause*]: She asked you to do that?

JACQUES

Yes.

D'AIGUINES

Did you do it?

JACQUES

Yes. [*Pause.*] You knew nothing about all that?

D'AIGUINES

I? Why, of course, I didn't!

JACQUES

Really! I had somehow imagined that you would have known about it.

D'AIGUINES

What are you driving at?

JACQUES

I merely wanted to let you know by what right I say what I shall have to say to you about her.

D'AIGUINES

That's all very well—but I've no right to listen to what you may have to say about the young lady. [*Rises.*]

JACQUES

Sit down, please.

D'AIGUINES

[*Disturbed*]: What for? I tell you again that it's something which doesn't concern me.

JACQUES

Steady! Otherwise, I'll be forced to think it's something which concerns you deeply.

D'AIGUINES

[*Feelingly*]: What do you mean?

JACQUES

I mean that a suspicion I had before your arrival has become a conviction in the last five minutes.

D'AIGUINES

All right—keep your suspicions to yourself, and allow me to leave?

JACQUES

[*Standing between the door and* D'AIGUINES]: I swear that you'll listen to me!

D'AIGUINES

Good God! Are you crazy?

JACQUES

No.

D'AIGUINES

You insist upon my listening to you?

JACQUES

[*Vehemently*]: Yes!

D'AIGUINES

You're wrong, I tell you!

JACQUES

We'll see as to that.

D'AIGUINES

Very well, I've warned you. Do as you like. . . .

JACQUES

I shan't take long, don't worry. If—contrary to what I think—what I have to say doesn't apply to you, at least you'll know to whom it should be repeated. When a man occupies in a girl's life the place which the person I'm referring to occupies in Irene's life—when he makes her do or lets her do what she has done in order not to be separated from him—he has no valid excuse, none, do you hear, for not marrying her. That is to say, if he's free. If he isn't, then he must take steps to become so, at no matter what cost and at the earliest possible moment. Now you have it.

D'AIGUINES

[*Pause*]: Is that all?

JACQUES

Well, just about. For I shouldn't like to think that the person in question were a man without honor. If that were the case then the duty of a friend is clear; to warn Montcel to protect his daughter. But I hope it won't be necessary to go to that extreme.

D'AIGUINES

Have you quite finished this time?

JACQUES

Yes.

D'AIGUINES

Then, unless I'm crazy I must conclude that you believe me to be Mademoiselle de Montcel's lover or something of the sort. That's it, isn't it?

JACQUES

That is the most likely supposition, yes. . . .

D'AIGUINES

[*Earnestly*]: Well, then look at me and despite the high strung condition you seem to be in, try to see things clearly. I give you my word of honor that you're mistaken. I am not and never have been anything but an acquaintance of hers, do you hear . . . not even a friend. You can believe me or not, that's your affair. That's all I've got to say. And please understand that if I've taken the trouble of replying to you at all instead of treating you like a lunatic and leaving here without a word, it's solely because of our old friendship.

JACQUES

[*Impressed by* D'AIGUINES' *truthful attitude, but despairing*]: Then . . . who is it?

D'AIGUINES

How should I know? . . . *Has* she a lover?

JACQUES

Yes.

D'AIGUINES

Did she tell you so?

JACQUES

She let me believe it—which amounts to the same thing.

D'AIGUINES

Not always. You may be too hasty in drawing conclusions.

JACQUES

Well, it's the only possible explanation. If it weren't true, she'd have said so. She couldn't have doubted for a moment that I was convinced of it.

D'AIGUINES

[*Pause*]: Well, in any case, I'm sorry, but I can give you no information. And if you've nothing more to say. . . .

JACQUES

You're not going?

D'AIGUINES

I must. I came as soon as I got your note but I'm leaving Paris in a few days and I've a great deal to do.

JACQUES

Don't go, I beg you! You're the only one who can help me find this man and I *must* find him.

D'AIGUINES

But since I know nothing—

JACQUES

That's not possible! You must have some idea, some suspicion. Seeing her constantly . . . knowing the sort of life she leads . . . whom she sees. . . .

D'AIGUINES

But you're wrong. I don't see her constantly. Once in a while she goes out with us—but I've much less in common with her than you seem to think—

JACQUES

How can that be? You're almost the only people she ever sees—she spends all her time at your house. You can't help knowing *something!*

D'AIGUINES

[*Coldly, not looking at* JACQUES]: I know nothing.

JACQUES

I don't believe you!

D'AIGUINES

See here! That's quite enough—

JACQUES

I believed you a moment ago, believed you without proof, when you said you were not her lover. You were telling the truth then. Now, you're not, you're lying. You're lying so as not to betray the secret of some one who is probably your friend. That's it, isn't it?

D'AIGUINES

I know nothing.

JACQUES

Listen: just tell me that he's a decent chap and that he'll marry her—and I'll ask you nothing more.

D'AIGUINES

I have nothing to say. I know nothing.

JACQUES

But don't you understand that this poor girl must be saved, that she can't be allowed to go more deeply every day into an affair that is ruining her! . . . And if it were only that! She has already begun to suffer. What's going on? . . . Has she felt that he wants to be rid of her? I don't know. But what

I *do* know is that she spends her time locked in her room, sobbing. That's what she has come to!

D'AIGUINES

Oh! . . . [*Gesture.*]

JACQUES

That doesn't worry you, eh? Well it does me! I'd give my life, do you hear, my life, to make her happy.

D'AIGUINES

[*Looks at him in surprise.*]: You mean to say you love her?

JACQUES

I am her friend.

D'AIGUINES

Answer me. One doesn't do what you have done out of mere friendship—nor go through with a thing like this pretended engagement. You love her?

JACQUES

Very well, then, I do love her. I've loved her for ten years, and I'll never love any one else. What of it?

D'AIGUINES

You love her? Is that true?

JACQUES

Yes!

D'AIGUINES

Then for Christ's sake, get away from here! Get away! It doesn't matter where—as far as you can and stay away as long as you can! Don't come back until you're cured! That's all I can say!

JACQUES

What do you mean?

D'AIGUINES

I'm giving you some advice, good advice, that's all.

JACQUES

You're going to explain to me exactly what you mean! Aren't you?

D'AIGUINES

[*With hesitation*]: Why—there's nothing to explain— You love this young woman and from what you tell me I gather she loves some one else. That being the case, the best thing to do is clear out. Don't you agree with me?

JACQUES

Clear out and leave her in the hands of some rotter, probably—some rotter who wanted her and so made her believe he'd marry her.

D'AIGUINES

Is she really so simple as that?

JACQUES

A woman is always that the first time she's in love. This is her first experience, I have reasons to know that. If she had loved any one before this, I'd probably have been the man. I adored her and until last year I lived in the hope that some day she'd be my wife. And she would have been, do you hear, if this other man hadn't appeared. I didn't fight against it, there was no use. But since he's been the means of making me unhappy, at least I want him to be the means of making her happy. To do that I must find him.

D'AIGUINES

You can do nothing for her.

JACQUES

How do you know?

D'AIGUINES

No one can do anything for her.

JACQUES

Why? [D'AIGUINES *gestures, but remains silent.*] Ah! You made a slip there! You're not going to keep on pretending that you don't know how things are! You can't keep silent any longer!

D'AIGUINES

Leave her alone! Don't meddle in this, believe me! And don't ask me anything more!

JACQUES

Look here, you don't suppose I'm going to be satisfied with vague warnings that can have only one effect: making me more anxious than ever! I'm not asking for advice, I'm demanding a name!

D'AIGUINES

[*Abruptly*]: The name of her lover? She has no lover! Now, are you satisfied?

JACQUES

What?

D'AIGUINES

It might be better for her if she had one!

JACQUES

I don't understand.

Photograph by Florence Vandamm

D'AIGUINES: It is not only a *man* who may be dangerous to a woman. . . . In some cases it can be another woman.

(BASIL RATHBONE *and* ARTHUR WONTNER)

D'AIGUINES

A woman can free herself from a lover—even if he's the worst scoundrel living. She can get over it. Whereas in *her* case—

JACQUES

In her case, what? Finish!

D'AIGUINES

Hers is quite another kind of bondage. . . . And that kind—[*Gesture.*]

JACQUES

Another kind of bondage?

D'AIGUINES

Yes. It is not only a *man* who may be dangerous to a woman. . . . In some cases it can be another woman.

JACQUES

Another *woman?*

D'AIGUINES

Yes.

JACQUES

What are you talking about? You mean to say it's on account of a woman that Irene refused to go with her father to Rome?

D'AIGUINES

Yes.

JACQUES

It's on account of a *woman* that she spends her time crying?

D'AIGUINES

Yes.

JACQUES

What kind of story is this?

D'AIGUINES

The kind of story that often happens—regardless of what men think. The kind of story that people don't believe for the most part, or which makes them smile, half amused and half indulgent.

JACQUES

But it's impossible! Irene is much too well balanced.

D'AIGUINES

What does that prove?

JACQUES

Are you positive of this?

D'AIGUINES

Yes.

JACQUES

Do you—know this woman?

D'AIGUINES

Yes. [*Looks at* JACQUES *quickly, and sees that the latter is not observing him. A great sadness crosses his face.*] I know her.

JACQUES

[*After a moment*]: I am dumbfounded—

D'AIGUINES

And a little relieved . . . aren't you?

JACQUES

Well, good Lord! After what I had feared! . . .

D'AIGUINES

So you'd prefer—? [*Pause.*] Well, you're wrong to prefer it!

JACQUES

You'd rather she had a lover?

D'AIGUINES

In your place? Yes! A hundred, a thousand times rather!

JACQUES

Are you mad?

D'AIGUINES

It's you who are mad. If she had a lover I'd say to you: Patience, my boy, patience and courage. Your cause isn't lost. No man lasts forever in a woman's life. You love her and she'll come back to you if you know how to wait. . . . But in this case I say: Don't wait! There's no use. She'll never return—and if ever your paths should cross again fly from her, fly from her . . . do you hear? Otherwise you are lost! Otherwise you'll spend your existence pursuing a phantom which you can never overtake. One can never overtake them! They are shadows. They must be left to dwell alone among themselves in the kingdom of shadows! Don't go near them . . . they're a menace! Above all, never try to be anything to them, no matter how little—that's where the danger lies. For, after all, they have some need of us in their lives . . . it isn't always easy for a woman to get along. So if a man offers to help her, to share with her what he has, and to give her his name, naturally she accepts. What difference can it make to her? So long as he doesn't exact love, she's not concerned about the rest. Only, can you imagine the existence of a man if he has the misfortune to love—to adore a *shadow* near whom he lives? Tell me, can you imagine what that's like? Take my word for it, old man, it's a rotten life! One's used up quickly by that game. One gets old in no time—and at thirty-five, look for yourself, one's hair is gray!

JACQUES

Do you mean—?

D'AIGUINES

Yes. And I hope you'll profit by my example. Understand this: they are not for us. They must be shunned, left alone. Don't make my mistake. Don't say, as I said in a situation almost like yours, don't say: "Oh, it's nothing but a sort of ardent friendship—an affectionate intimacy . . . nothing very serious . . . we know all about that sort of thing!" No! We don't know *anything* about it! We can't begin to know what it is. It's mysterious—terrible! Friendship, yes—that's the mask. Under cover of friendship a woman can enter any household, whenever and however she pleases—at any hour of the day—she can poison and pillage everything before the man whose home she destroys is even aware of what's happening to him. When finally he realizes things it's too late—he is alone! Alone in the face of a secret alliance of two beings who understand one another because they're alike, because they're of the same sex, because they're of a different planet than he, the stranger, the enemy! Ah! if a *man* tries to steal your woman you can defend yourself, you can fight him on even terms, you can smash his face in. But in this case—there's nothing to be done—but *get out* while you still have strength to do it! And that's what you've got to do!

JACQUES

. . . Why don't you get out yourself?

D'AIGUINES

Oh, with me it's different. I can't leave her now. We've been married eight years. Where would she go? . . . Besides it's too late. I couldn't live without her any more. What can I do—I love her? . . . [*Pause.*] You've never seen her? [JACQUES *shakes his head.*] You'd understand better if you knew her. She has all the feminine allurements, every one. As soon as one is near her, one feels—how shall I say it—a sort of deep charm. Not only I feel it. Every one feels it. But I more than the rest because I live near her. I really believe she is the most harmonious being that has ever breathed. . . . Sometimes when I'm away from her, I have the strength to hate her for all the harm she has done me . . . but, with her, I don't struggle. I look at her . . . I listen to her . . . I worship her. You see?

JACQUES

[*Pursuing an idea*]: Tell me . . . why is Irene suffering?

D'AIGUINES

I don't know. [*Rises.*] You don't suppose I'm confided in, do you? She is suffering probably, as the weak always do, struggling with a stronger nature until they give in.

JACQUES

You think Irene is weak?

D'AIGUINES

Compared to the other? Oh, yes. [*Pause.*] She is probably still struggling.

JACQUES

Ah! [*Pause.*] So that's why she is unhappy? [*Rises.*]

D'AIGUINES

For that reason—or some other. She has many to choose from.

JACQUES

You mean—?

D'AIGUINES

Why shouldn't she suffer? I suffer, don't I?

JACQUES

That's not the same thing.

D'AIGUINES

You think so, do you? Well, on the contrary, I believe it's very much the same thing. There's only one way to love, you see, and one way to suffer. It's the same formula for everybody—and in that respect she and I have been in the same boat for some time. Only she hasn't got used to it yet—and I have.

JACQUES

I don't quite follow you.

D'AIGUINES

Haven't you heard any mention of a cruise?

JACQUES

A cruise?

D'AIGUINES

Yes. In the Mediterranean . . . on a yacht, an American yacht?

JACQUES

No. [*Pause.*] Is she to be one of the party?

D'AIGUINES

I don't know. That's why I'm asking if she spoke of it.

JACQUES

She never speaks to me of anything.

D'AIGUINES

In her place—I'd refuse to go.

JACQUES

You would?

D'AIGUINES

I doubt that she'll be able to refuse. However—that's her affair. What matters most is you. What are you going to do? Will you take my advice and go away for a while?

JACQUES

I don't know yet. I'll think it over.

D'AIGUINES

Don't wait, Jacques. Believe me.

JACQUES

It's not as dangerous for me as you think. I almost never see her.

D'AIGUINES

What difference does that make? When she needs you, she knows where to find you—you've seen that for yourself. That is how one can get caught, even after one has been warned. Remember what I'm telling you.

JACQUES

But where can I go?

D'AIGUINES

Anywhere—so long as it's far away. [*Pause.*] Have you still got your business interests in Morocco?

JACQUES

Yes, but—

D'AIGUINES

Then go back there for a while. At that distance she won't be able to turn to you so easily.

JACQUES

If you knew her as well as I do, you'd realize that you're needlessly alarmed. She turned to me for help in a moment of frenzy. But she's much too proud to do so again. Besides, I don't see how I could help her any more.

D'AIGUINES

How can you tell? [*Pause.*] If you don't want to go away, then find a woman that is attractive to you, a real woman. See if she can't make you forget the other one.

JACQUES

I've already tried that.

D'AIGUINES

And it didn't succeed? [JACQUES *shakes his head.*] You see my fears were not so exaggerated as you thought. There is nothing for you to do but go away—and without a moment's delay. Now it's up to you. [*Picks up his hat and gloves and offers* JACQUES *his hand. A bell is heard.*] Are you expecting some one?

JACQUES

No.

D'AIGUINES

Well, anyhow, I must be off—good-by, Jacques. [*They shake hands.*]

JACQUES

Thanks. . . .

D'AIGUINES

Oh! [*Gesture.*] If only I could have convinced you! [GEORGES *enters.*]

JACQUES

What is it?

GEORGES

Mademoiselle de Montcel would like to know if you can see her.

JACQUES

What!

GEORGES

And I said that I would see if you were in, monsieur.

JACQUES

[*Glances at* D'AIGUINES.] Ask her to wait in the salon, then close the door that gives into the hall.

GEORGES

Very good, monsieur.

JACQUES

It's Mademoiselle Irene?

GEORGES

Yes, monsieur.

JACQUES

Oh! Show Monsieur d'Aiguines out when he leaves. [GEORGES *exits.*] Well! This is an unexpected visit!

D'AIGUINES

Tell me—you've no intention, I hope, of repeating a word of what we've said to Mademoiselle de Montcel, have you?

JACQUES

Do you suppose she'd ever forgive me for knowing?

D'AIGUINES

Right! And now—good luck, old man. Remember—she can never belong to you no matter how you try. They're not for us. [*He exits and* JACQUES *stands a moment in the doorway, then crosses to salon door and opens it.*] Come in!

IRENE

[*Entering*]: You're sure I'm not disturbing you? [*Closes door.*]

JACQUES

Very sure.

IRENE

You'd tell me if I were, wouldn't you?

JACQUES

I'd tell you.

IRENE

Then may I stay? It won't bother you?

JACQUES

It won't bother me.

IRENE

[*She sits on the sofa*]: Were you surprised when you heard it was I?

JACQUES

[*Sitting at his desk and lighting the lamp*]: A little, yes.

IRENE

You wondered what I had come here for, didn't you?

JACQUES

I thought that no doubt there was something you wanted to talk to me about.

IRENE

There is.

JACQUES

Well, I'm listening.

IRENE

[*Smiling*]: Oh, please not like that. Don't speak

to me like a lawyer to his client. Be kind, affectionate! . . . Do change that severe look!

JACQUES

Why do you say I have a severe look?

IRENE

You always have a severe look, nowadays.

JACQUES

You're mistaken—

IRENE

Be sweet, Jacques, won't you? Like old times! I'm terribly in need of your sympathy.

JACQUES

Really?

IRENE

Why do you say *really* like that?

JACQUES

For no reason. Go on, continue.

IRENE

Are you surprised I ask you to be kind . . . to be affectionate . . . to me?

JACQUES

I've stopped being surprised by you, my dear—

IRENE

Don't be cruel! . . . I've given you the right to be, I don't forget that! But just the same I hope you won't be, do you mind? Not to-day, anyway. [*She turns her face away to hide tears.*]

JACQUES

[*More gently*]: What's the matter?

IRENE

Nothing. Pay no attention. [*Pause.*] Jacques, I want you to tell me something.

JACQUES

What?

IRENE

Since I asked you to—since you agreed to play this part to my father—have you no longer as much affection for me?

JACQUES

Why do you ask me that?

IRENE

Because I must know.

JACQUES

I have as much affection, only—

IRENE

Only?

JACQUES

It is no longer the same affection. I used to admire you. Now, I pity you.

IRENE

[*Pensive, without looking at him*]: And you despise me?

JACQUES

I pity you.

IRENE

You're right . . . I am to be pitied. But I can still count on you as a friend, can't I?

JACQUES

Yes.

IRENE

I need to believe that, to feel sure of it. You don't know, Jacques, how much you mean to me.

JACQUES

As much as that? [*Rises.*]

IRENE

Please, no sarcasm. You say you pity me. Then prove it.

JACQUES

How?

IRENE

Oh! . . . By showing me a little tenderness and being a little lenient, that's all.

JACQUES

Aren't you happy?

IRENE

Happy?

JACQUES

Yes.

IRENE

There are times when I wish I were dead.

JACQUES

Well, that *is* a way out, but—

IRENE

You don't believe me?

JACQUES

I hope you're exaggerating—if one had to kill oneself every time he was unhappy—

IRENE

Oh! I'm not thinking of killing myself. It takes courage to die like that. And I haven't even any courage left. . . . I have nothing left. . . .

JACQUES

Yet, you got what you wanted. You had to stay in Paris at any cost. Well, here you are— Oh, talking of that, I meant to tell you that I must write to your father.

IRENE

To father?

JACQUES

Yes. It was understood that I was to let him know as soon as possible what my intentions were and I promised to do it. He's already been gone a month and I haven't written yet. . . . It's time I did.

IRENE

Must you?

JACQUES

I'll tell him that the business matters that were worrying me at the time of his departure are now in such bad shape that I'm in no position to make plans for the future— Does that seem all right to you?

IRENE

Just as you wish.

JACQUES

I'll add that I am going to Morocco to attend directly to my interests there.

IRENE

[*With great alarm.*] But it isn't true, is it—you're not going away?

JACQUES

Yes, probably.

IRENE

But why? Is it really because of business matters?

JACQUES

No.

IRENE

Well, then? . . . Oh! You're not going alone?

JACQUES

What do you mean, not alone?

IRENE

Is some one going with you?

JACQUES

No, nobody.

IRENE

Then why must you go?

JACQUES

I need a change. This climate's not agreeing with me. I should have gone long ago—a year ago when you came back from Italy. Perhaps I'd have been better by now.

IRENE

It's because of me that you're going.

JACQUES

Good Lord!

IRENE

Is it true?

JACQUES

Don't you think it's about time that I considered my own peace of mind a little? After all I can't spend my life loving you and beginning to suffer all over again each time I see you.

IRENE

Then you still love me, Jacques? Is it true?

JACQUES

Does that surprise you?

IRENE

After what you must have believed of me lately, I was certain that was over . . . that you didn't love me any more. I felt it,—but I hoped it wasn't true.

JACQUES

You hoped it wasn't true?

IRENE

Yes.

JACQUES

You hoped that I still loved you?

IRENE

Yes.

JACQUES

[*Pause*]: I can't understand you.

IRENE

[*Looking away from him*]: Don't go away, Jacques.

JACQUES

What do you say?

IRENE

Don't go away. [JACQUES *looks at her, stupefied.*]

JACQUES

Ah, yes! You're afraid your father'll send for you when he receives my letter and learns I'm no longer here, eh? Well, I'm sorry, but this time you'll have to manage without me. You can do what you like and how you like, but I shall write to your father to-night.

IRENE

[*Shrugging her shoulders*]: Write all you want to. I don't care!

JACQUES

[*Sarcastically*]: Really!

IRENE

Absolutely, I swear to you!

JACQUES

[*Puzzled*]: Then why don't you want me to go away?

IRENE

Oh! . . . for no reason at all. [*She rises.*]

JACQUES

Sit down again and answer me.

IRENE

It's no use. Go, go away—since you're in such a hurry to forget me! Go!

JACQUES

Really, Irene, what is this game you're playing now?

IRENE

Please forgive me. I don't know what I'm saying any more. Oh, Jacques, I'm so miserable! [*She falls into a chair and cries.*]

JACQUES

[*Touched, going to her*]: What's the matter?

IRENE

[*Clinging to him*]: You mustn't leave me. I'm so alone, so wretched! Jacques! Only you can save me!

JACQUES

But what do you want me to do?

IRENE

Protect me! Shield me!

JACQUES

Shield you?

IRENE

Yes.

JACQUES

I assure you, Irene, I'm doing my best to understand you, but really—

IRENE

I know, I must seem crazy. Well, I am crazy! You have got to treat me like a crazy person—a sick person—and take care of me, that's all. If you don't come to my rescue right away—it will be too late!

JACQUES

Are you in danger of something?

IRENE

Yes.

JACQUES

An imminent danger?

IRENE

Yes.

JACQUES

Can't you tell me what it is?

IRENE

[*After hesitating*]: It's about a cruise, my going away—and I mustn't go. I don't want to go—if I do, it's all over. I'd be lost!

JACQUES

What is forcing you to go?

IRENE

Ah! I am afraid of myself.

JACQUES

Then why don't you take a train to Rome with Gisele to join your father?

IRENE

I had thought of that. . . . But at the last minute I wouldn't go—I wouldn't have the strength—

JACQUES

Yes, you would! I'll help if you wish.

IRENE

[*Shaking her head*]: Or else I'd come back.

JACQUES

No!

IRENE

You see, there are times in which I can see clearly, such as now, when I am sane and free to use my own mind. . . . But there are other times when I can't, when I don't know what I'm doing. It's like—a prison to which I must return captive, despite myself. I'm—I'm—

JACQUES

Fascinated?

IRENE

Yes! I need some one to watch me, to hold me back. Some one who has understood or guessed certain things—that I can't talk about, that I can never tell!

JACQUES

Is that what you expect of me? How can I restrain you from doing what you want to do? Have I the least influence over you? Have you ever listened to my advice? Please remember that it was only a month ago you rejected it.

IRENE

It's no longer the same.

JACQUES

What is no longer the same?

IRENE

Many things. I will listen to you now. I want to listen to you.

JACQUES

But you won't be able to! You won't be allowed to! What weapons have I to fight with? What can I add to what you yourself have said? You acknowledge that this cruise would be your ruin? What can I add to that? And then do you imagine for one moment that advice from me would hold you back during one of those hours of insensibility you speak of? [IRENE *shakes head.*] You see! . . . And surely you don't expect me to hold you by force, do you? So, what can I do for you?

IRENE

Everything. You can save me.

JACQUES

How?

IRENE

You are the only one who can save me—

JACQUES

Why?

IRENE

Because you love me—

JACQUES

It's for that very reason that I can do nothing. As soon as I saw you miserable, I'd be useless. You can't take as your trained nurse a man who loves you!

IRENE

Not as a trained nurse—

JACQUES

Well, what then?

IRENE

[*Looking at him*]: Jacques—would you like me to give myself to you?

JACQUES

Irene!

IRENE

Would you?

JACQUES

Don't!

IRENE

Jacques?

JACQUES

So that's it. That's what you've come to offer me?

IRENE

[*Lowering head*]: Yes.

JACQUES

My poor Irene.

IRENE

You don't want me?

JACQUES

[*Faces her*]: But I love you! Don't you understand what that means?

IRENE

Of course—

JACQUES

[*Forcibly*]: You offer me your body, your poor body as a pledge, is that it? You want to soil it with me so that you can tell this woman—

IRENE

[*With a cry*]: Jacques!

JACQUES

[*Still moved*]: Yes, I know! I've guessed it! What of it? I suppose you want to tell her that you've given yourself to a man, so that she'll leave you alone? But as for me, me—it's not your body I want. It's you, all of you, don't you see? Can you give me that—tell me? Can you give that to some one you don't love? For, after all, you don't love me, do you? You don't love me?

IRENE

[*With despair*]: I want so much to love you. [*She bends over and sobs, her head on his breast.*]

JACQUES

[*Distraught*]: Poor child!

IRENE

[*Through her tears*]: You think that I don't know it would mean my happiness? I know only too well that the place I really belong is here against your shoulder. Why won't you let me stay here?

JACQUES

Oh! Irene,—what you are asking is too terrible.

IRENE

Why? . . . Perhaps I would learn to love you?

JACQUES

Afterwards, you mean? No, my dear. . . .

IRENE

But once you told me that I would.

JACQUES

Ah! Because at that time I thought that only your pride stood between us. I didn't know then all that separates us!

IRENE

But when you will have cured me. . . .

JACQUES

Do you really believe that I could?

IRENE

Yes, if you're very kind, very indulgent, if you have a little patience.

JACQUES

But, you see I love you too much for that.

IRENE

Then . . . you refuse me? . . . Is that it, Jacques? . . . What is going to become of me!

JACQUES

What would become of me? I've been hurt enough as it is.

IRENE

But that's over, I won't hurt you any more. How could I hurt you when it will be you who have saved me?

JACQUES

That means nothing. You wouldn't do it on purpose, naturally.

IRENE

Jacques, look at me. Look in my eyes. [*Pause.*] I will give you everything a man can expect from the woman he loves.

JACQUES

[*Disturbed*]: Irene! I have dreamed of that too long.

IRENE

Take me in your arms. I am yours, Jacques, all of me. . . .

JACQUES

You don't realize what you're promising.

IRENE

Yes, I do.

JACQUES

There is still time . . . you can still go.

IRENE

I am not afraid.

JACQUES

You really wish it? Are you sure that you do?

IRENE

Yes.

JACQUES

[*Taking her in his arms*]: Irene? . . . Is it true?

[*He starts to kiss her on the mouth. As* IRENE *beholds his face filled with longing, she makes an abrupt movement of aversion. He lets her go.*]

You see?

IRENE

No, no—forgive me!

[*This time it is she who offers her lips to him. Then, her nerves giving way, she lets her head fall on his shoulder, struggles with herself a moment, and breaks into tears.*]

Photograph by Florence Vandamm

JACQUES: You see?
(BASIL RATHBONE *and* HELEN MENKEN)

JACQUES

[*In despair*]: Irene!

IRENE

No, no!—Pay no attention!—It doesn't mean anything. . . . It's all over! You will keep me with you? Always?

JACQUES

I'll try.

THE CURTAIN FALLS

THE CAPTIVE

ACT THREE

SCENE: *The same as Act Two. A year after.*

JACQUES *is seated alone, smoking and meditating.* GEORGES, *his man, enters at back, bringing a letter which he gives to* JACQUES. *The latter inspects the envelope and seems surprised.*

JACQUES

Who brought this letter?

GEORGES

A maid, monsieur. She is waiting for an answer.

[*He walks to back and waits near the door.* JACQUES *opens and reads the letter. After a few moments of thought, he rises, crosses to his desk, takes a sheet of paper and starts writing.*]

JACQUES

For what time did madame order the car?

GEORGES

Three o'clock, monsieur.

[JACQUES *looks at watch, finishes letter, slips it into an envelope and hands it to* GEORGES.]

JACQUES

There.

[GEORGES *goes out.* JACQUES *again picks up the letter he has received, re-reads it, then carries it to his nose, inhales its scent and smiles.* IRENE *appears at the right.* JACQUES *puts letter in his pocket. Her hat is on and she is ready to go out. She has in her hand a bundle of samples of materials for hangings.*]

IRENE

You didn't tell me which of these samples you preferred. This one—this—or that?

JACQUES

It's for your own room. You'd better choose it yourself.

IRENE

But I want you to like it.

JACQUES

I'll like whichever one you choose.

IRENE

Well, at least you might tell me which one you prefer.

JACQUES

But I approve your choice in advance—

IRENE

Oh! How annoying of you!

JACQUES

Are you going out?

IRENE

Yes, I must go to the decorator's, and to the painter's. Then at three-thirty, I have an appointment at Praxine's studio to have another look at the little landscape that I saw the other day. Don't you want to come?

JACQUES

I can't.

IRENE

You'll have to see it some time.

JACQUES

What for?

IRENE

I'm certainly not going to buy a picture as expensive as that without your having seen it.

JACQUES

You don't need my advice. I don't know anything about painting. If you like the picture, buy it, that's all.

IRENE

Can't you really come? I'll pass by here with the car and pick you up. It won't take more than twenty minutes altogether.

JACQUES

I can't, I tell you. I'm waiting for some one.

IRENE

Who?

JACQUES

Oh, just—a caller.

IRENE

At what time?

JACQUES

At half-past three.

IRENE

Will it take long?

JACQUES

That I don't know. [*Telephone rings. He rises, takes up receiver.*] Hullo . . . yes . . . who is it please? . . . Oh! Just a minute. [*To* IRENE.] Praxine wants to speak to you.

IRENE

[*At telephone*]: Hullo . . . Oh, hullo, how do you do? . . . Why of course I haven't forgotten . . . at half-past three, yes. . . . All right! . . . What? . . . No, he is so sorry, but he has an appointment and won't be able to come. I'll be there. [*She hangs up receiver.*] He asked me to be on time, because he has to leave. [*Pause.*] Well then?

JACQUES

Well then what?

IRENE

May I really buy the picture if I still like it as much as I did?

JACQUES

Why, of course.

IRENE

You're a darling. But, you know, I really think it's a good buy. Praxine never gets less than twenty-five thousand francs for his smallest canvases and he's giving me this for fifteen thousand—just because it's I.

JACQUES

That's splendid.

IRENE

I do so hope you'll like it, but I warn you, it's extremely modern. You may think it's horrible—

JACQUES

Of course I won't. What time will you be back?

IRENE

Oh, not late. I have to stop and send some books to Gisele; she writes me she has nothing to read. That's all. I'll be back here for tea.

JACQUES

If by any chance the person I'm expecting should still be here when you return, would you mind not coming in?

IRENE

No, of course not.

JACQUES

I'd rather you didn't meet.

IRENE

Oh! Why not?

JACQUES

I don't think either you or she would enjoy it much.

IRENE

Ah! [*Pause.*] Can't you tell me who it is?

JACQUES

Does it interest you?

IRENE

Well, really!—After what you've just told me—

JACQUES

It's a very charming woman, towards whom I've behaved very shabbily.

IRENE

[*Searching in her mind*]: A woman towards whom—Madame Meillant?

JACQUES

Exactly.

IRENE

No? How funny!

JACQUES

Isn't it?

IRENE

She's coming to see you?

JACQUES

I wrote, asking her to call. Whether she'll come or not, I don't know.

IRENE

But why is she coming?

JACQUES

Here. [*He hands her the letter he has just received.*]

IRENE

[*After having read it*]: What are the letters she mentions?

JACQUES

The letters she wrote me while—that she wrote me last year.

IRENE

Hadn't you given them back to her?

JACQUES

No. We left Paris in such a hurry a year ago that I didn't have time, and since our return I haven't given it a thought.

IRENE

[*Smiling*]: Poor thing. [*Gives him back letter.*]

JACQUES

[*Putting it on the desk*]: You don't mind my receiving her here?

IRENE

Why no, not at all.

JACQUES

That's what I thought.

IRENE

Why should I mind?

JACQUES

For no reason, that's true.

IRENE

I have perfect confidence in you.

JACQUES

Of course.

IRENE

I suppose you wanted to give her the letters yourself, and you're quite right.

JACQUES

Naturally.

IRENE

[*Looking at him*]: What's the matter?

JACQUES

Nothing.

IRENE

You look annoyed that I should be taking this so amiably.

JACQUES

I? On the contrary, I'm delighted.

IRENE

Would you rather have me jealous?

JACQUES

I repeat that I'm delighted.

IRENE

I have no reason for being jealous, have I?

JACQUES

No! Absolutely—none.

IRENE

Well, then?

JACQUES

Jealousy in your case would certainly be uncalled for.

IRENE

Meaning what?

JACQUES

Simply, that just as jealousy's the most natural thing in the world when one's in love, it becomes meaningless when one isn't, that's all.

IRENE

So—I don't love you?

JACQUES

Of course you don't love me.

IRENE

How absurd!

JACQUES

What is absurd?

IRENE

To say that.

JACQUES

Not at all, why is it?

IRENE

Come now, what are you reproaching me about?

JACQUES

I'm not reproaching you about anything.

IRENE

Have you any fault to find with me?

JACQUES

No. Go along and do your errands. Please!

IRENE

No, let's clear this up. I'd prefer that. [*Removes her coat and puts it on divan.*]

JACQUES

What for? It's so useless.

IRENE

If I've disappointed you in any way, tell me.

JACQUES

In no way.

IRENE

Don't I do all that I can to make you happy?

JACQUES

All that you can.

IRENE

Have I had any other thought than your happiness, since I've been your wife? Has my life had any other purpose? Don't I always ask myself, before doing anything, if you'll be pleased and whether you'll approve?

JACQUES

Even in choosing your bedroom curtains,—quite right.

IRENE

Don't make fun of me, please.

JACQUES

I'm not making fun of you. You're an attentive, devoted and faithful wife. What more can I ask? If all that doesn't make me happy, I must be very hard to please.

IRENE

I don't understand you any more, Jacques.

JACQUES

I know it! That's why all this talk can accomplish nothing.

IRENE

[*Pause*]: Then—then you're not happy?

JACQUES

In any case, it's not your fault. I repeat that I have no reproaches to make.

IRENE

[*Wearily*]: But what can I do, then?

JACQUES

Nothing. There's nothing to be done.

IRENE

Yet you have my every thought. You know that, don't you?

JACQUES

No. I don't know that at all.

IRENE

You don't?

JACQUES

How do you expect me to know what your thoughts are? They're yours. They're no business of mine.

IRENE

But I hide nothing from you. Nothing that might disturb you—I swear it.

JACQUES

As to that— [*A gesture of futility.*]

IRENE

You don't believe me? Well, then, question me. I'd much rather have that.

JACQUES

No, no—no questions! Let's leave in the dark what was meant to be in the dark.

IRENE

No! Since we've come to this, I want you to question me! Perhaps you'll see how unjust you are when you know everything.

JACQUES

Then there are things to know?

IRENE

Only things that can reassure you.

JACQUES

Tell me. I'm listening. [*Pause.*] Have you seen her again?

IRENE

No.

JACQUES

Has she telephoned you?

IRENE

No.

JACQUES

Written?

IRENE

Yes.

JACQUES

When?

IRENE

Shortly after our return to Paris. [*Pause.*] Twice.

JACQUES

Where are the letters?

IRENE

[*Simply*]: I sent them back unopened.

JACQUES

Unopened?

IRENE

Word of honor.

JACQUES

How did you send them back?

IRENE

By the person who brought them.

JACQUES

How does it happen that I didn't know about it?

IRENE

You weren't in. You had gone out.

JACQUES

Both times?

IRENE

Yes.

JACQUES

They probably waited for me to leave before bringing them!

IRENE

Perhaps. I don't know.

JACQUES

Then you've no idea what she wanted of you?

IRENE

Oh,—to see me again, no doubt.

JACQUES

What makes you think that?

IRENE

I'm just supposing it.

JACQUES

Is that all?

IRENE

No.

JACQUES

What else?

IRENE

A few days after the second letter came her maid spoke to me in the street.

JACQUES

Perfect!

IRENE

It wasn't—she, who had sent her.

JACQUES

[*Ironically*]: Really?

IRENE

No. She was very ill.

JACQUES

[*Same tone*]: Well, well,

IRENE

She'd been ill a long time. She had just had a relapse. All that night she'd been delirious. It seems . . . that she had asked for me several times. . . . So the maid thought it best to come and tell me.

JACQUES

And then? What did you do?

IRENE

Nothing.

JACQUES

Nothing?

IRENE

[*Shaking her head*]: I merely asked the maid to bring me news of her the next day. The next day the news was better. I told her not to come back.

JACQUES

[*Pause*]: And then?

IRENE

That's all.

JACQUES

Absolutely?

IRENE

Yes.

JACQUES

Why haven't you told me this before?

IRENE

I didn't want to worry you unnecessarily. You're so sensitive, you'd have been agitated despite anything I could say. I decided to wait a few days and then tell you.

JACQUES

Why a few days?

IRENE

She's going to Switzerland for several months to rest. I wanted to wait until she had gone.

JACQUES

Who told you she was going? The maid?

IRENE

Yes. [*Pause.*] Aren't you a little reassured now?

JACQUES

I wasn't worried.

IRENE

You know you can have confidence in me?

JACQUES

But I've always had confidence in you, Irene. I never doubted that when the time came, you would act as you did. You promised when you married me never to see that woman again. I was certain that you never would see her again.

IRENE

Then what's on your mind? Why aren't you happy?

JACQUES

And you, are you happy?

IRENE

I? [*Pause.*] Of course I'm happy.

JACQUES

Oh! Come now!

IRENE

[*Going toward him*]: But really, Jacques! . . . Haven't I everything to make me happy? We have all we need, we get along so well—you're kindness and generosity itself to me. What more can I wish for?

JACQUES

Why do you try to make me believe that nothing is lacking in your life?

IRENE

Because it's true!

JACQUES

No, it's not true!— You're not yet thirty and I'm not thirty-five. Happiness, at our age, doesn't consist in leading a comfortable existence . . . a string of pearls—a couple of cars. It's too soon for that. It's love that's lacking, Irene; you long to love, just as I long to be loved.

IRENE

What do you want me to say? You've convinced yourself that I don't love you—

JACQUES

Ah, if you knew how hard it's been to convince myself of it. The stupidly hopeful stages I went through! I've clung desperately to the substitutes of love—from tenderness and friendship to the most pathetic of all—compliance. On a word or a gesture that I could interpret in terms of my desire I'd regain confidence. Those illusions are gone. I know that I can really mean nothing to you. I'm as incapable of making you happy as of making you unhappy. . . . Oh, God! if only I could make you suffer!

IRENE

You can.

JACQUES

How?

IRENE

By continuing to say these silly things!

JACQUES

You know as well as I that they're not silly. Why shut your eyes to it? Listen, do you know why I've made an appointment with Madame Meillant?

IRENE

Why, Jacques?

JACQUES

It was to see the effect it might have on you; whether you would object or seem annoyed. It made you laugh. That's the only result I got.

IRENE

Did you want me to weep?

JACQUES

I wanted to see just how far your indifference went.

IRENE

Is it my fault if I believe in your love for me . . . if I don't fear your being unfaithful?

JACQUES

If you loved me, you would fear it. But the truth is, that it wouldn't matter to you in the least.

IRENE

That's not so!

JACQUES

Oh, yes, it is.

IRENE

It would hurt me a great deal?

JACQUES

Hurt you?

IRENE

Of course?

JACQUES

Tell me just how it would hurt you?

IRENE

How can I tell you that? I don't know.

JACQUES

Well, try to imagine.

IRENE

I'd be very disappointed, very saddened. I'd feel that—that afterwards I would not like to be taken in your arms again as I did before . . . there.

JACQUES

[*Looking at her mournfully*]: As you did before?

IRENE

Yes.

JACQUES

You really like so much to be in my arms? Tell me!

IRENE

[*Lowering her head*]: Why—yes.

JACQUES

My poor Irene—so you think me blind?

IRENE

[*Pause, then with an effort*]: Have I—have I ever refused you?

JACQUES

You've had a great deal of courage.

IRENE

I thought I made you happy—that was all I wanted.

JACQUES

One can't give happiness so easily as that.

IRENE

I'm sorry.

JACQUES

Love, you see—is something very different.

IRENE

Everything I could give you—I've given. If that doesn't suffice you—

JACQUES

No!

IRENE

Then, look somewhere else, that's all.

JACQUES

You'd like that, wouldn't you? What a deliverance for you that day would be!

IRENE

Oh! Jacques, that will do! [*Pause.*] And anyway, it's getting late and I must be going. [*Gets coat from divan, puts it on and goes toward door.*]

JACQUES

Irene?

IRENE

What?

JACQUES

Come here.

IRENE

What do you want?

JACQUES

Forgive me. I didn't mean—to hurt you. If I have, forgive me.

IRENE

[*Going towards him*]: Why are you so unjust?

JACQUES

Well, you see, I can't get used to it.

IRENE

Used to what? My not loving you? But I do. You are everything that I admire, everything that pleases me, everything that I respect in this world!

JACQUES

[*Dejected*]: Yes, I suppose so.

IRENE

Well, do you think that many wives can say as much of their husbands?

JACQUES

I wasn't asking for as much, either.

IRENE

Do I love any one else but you? I don't, do I? Well then? . . . If you had been told a year ago that you held the first and only place in my life, wouldn't you have been happy?

JACQUES

Of course.

IRENE

Do you think my feeling for you hasn't grown since I asked you to keep me here? You remember that day, don't you?

JACQUES

Yes.

IRENE

[*Smiling—comes close to him*]: And at Montcel, three weeks later, the mayor's speech and the little chapel, where it was so cold; you remember that too?

JACQUES

Yes.

IRENE

Do you regret what happened that day?

JACQUES

Do you?

IRENE

No.

JACQUES

That's something anyway.

IRENE

Then—will you kiss me?

JACQUES

You want me to?

IRENE

Yes,—I do. [*He takes her in his arms and holds her there a moment, quietly, looking at her. She leans forward to kiss him, her left arm is raised to clasp him, when her eyes rest on her wrist watch.*] Oh, look! Quarter to four! Can that be the time?

JACQUES

Yes.

IRENE

I had no idea! Oh! what a nuisance. Now I won't have time to go to the decorator's. Hurry, dearest!

JACQUES

What?

IRENE

Aren't you going to kiss me?

JACQUES

[*Drawing away*]: No, you're late already.

IRENE

It doesn't matter.

JACQUES

No, no—run along.

IRENE

Don't be silly! Just because I said. . . .

JACQUES

Go on. . . . Go— [*He turns his back to her and walks away.*]

IRENE

Great heavens, but you're touchy!

JACQUES

Please go!

IRENE

[*She sighs*]: See you later, then?

JACQUES

Yes. [IRENE *goes toward door. At the door she turns around.*]

IRENE

I hope you won't make love to that woman?

JACQUES

Thank you for thinking of it!

IRENE

You promise me you won't?

JACQUES

Yes, yes, of course. [IRENE *goes out at back.* JACQUES *sits down, thoughtful, a bitter expression on his face. After quite a pause, he sees on the desk the letter* FRANÇOISE *has written, takes it, puts it in his pocket, goes and opens a cabinet and takes out a rather bulky envelope, which he brings to the desk. He empties its contents: letters. He picks one at random and reads it. At that moment a bell is heard. He puts the letters back in the envelope.* GEORGES *enters.*]

GEORGES

Madame Meillant- monsieur.

JACQUES

Ask her to come in. [*Puts letters in desk drawer. A moment later* GEORGES *ushers* FRANÇOISE *into the room and retires.*] How are you, Françoise? It was sweet of you to come. [*He kisses her hand.*]

FRANÇOISE

Oh, I only came to get my letters. Don't imagine it was for any other reason.

JACQUES

I'm imagining nothing at all. But I may thank you for having come, mayn't I?

FRANÇOISE

Why didn't you give the maid the letters as I asked in my note? It would have been much simpler.

JACQUES

I preferred their passing directly from my hands into yours. It seemed to me the safest way. And after all, why not say it: I wanted to see you again.

FRANÇOISE

Really? And you didn't ask yourself if *I* wanted to see you?

JACQUES

I ventured to think that if that were too disagreeable you wouldn't come.

FRANÇOISE

I wanted my letters, I've just told you that. You don't seem to realize that I've been waiting for them a year.

JACQUES

They were here and I was circling the world. Unless I were to return especially from Japan to get them—

FRANÇOISE

You could have sent them to me before you left.

JACQUES

I didn't have the time.

FRANÇOISE

You left very hurriedly.

JACQUES

Very. But you weren't anxious about your letters, were you? You knew they were in safe-keeping.

FRANÇOISE

Oh, you think so? And suppose your wife had taken a fancy to search your desk?

JACQUES

That's quite unlikely.

FRANÇOISE

Just the same, such things do happen.

JACQUES

Not here.

FRANÇOISE

Then your wife isn't jealous?

JACQUES

Not at all.

FRANÇOISE

You're lucky! She's not in, I hope.

JACQUES

No, she's just gone out.

FRANÇOISE

[*Going to table and regarding picture of* IRENE]: Is this she?

JACQUES

Yes.

FRANÇOISE

My compliments.

JACQUES

Thanks.

FRANÇOISE

Why didn't you tell me the truth the last time I came here?

JACQUES

The truth?

FRANÇOISE

Yes; that you were going to be married. I should have preferred that, you know. It would have been nicer. Besides, at least it was a reason.

JACQUES

I didn't tell you because I didn't know it myself

FRANÇOISE

You didn't know it?

JACQUES

No.

FRANÇOISE

And three weeks later the papers announced that you were married!

JACQUES

Yes.

FRANÇOISE

You didn't lose much time, then?

JACQUES

Once a thing like that is decided upon. . . .

FRANÇOISE

She's a childhood friend, isn't she?

JACQUES

She's a cousin.

FRANÇOISE

First cousin?

JACQUES

No.

FRANÇOISE

Just as well!—And you've loved each other always, of course?

JACQUES

Well—

FRANÇOISE

Oh, you can tell me now. I really don't know why I'm asking you; it matters to me so little.

JACQUES

Then—

FRANÇOISE

Give me my letters, won't you?

JACQUES

Are you in such a hurry to get them?

FRANÇOISE

Yes.

JACQUES

Why?

FRANÇOISE

Because.

JACQUES

I'm not asking you for mine!

FRANÇOISE

I burned them long ago.

JACQUES

Really?

FRANÇOISE

Besides, for all the letters *you* ever sent—and for all they ever said—

JACQUES

Just the same, it wasn't very nice to burn them.

FRANÇOISE

Why should I have kept them?

JACQUES

To re-read them now and then.

FRANÇOISE

I had other things to do.

JACQUES

Ah?

FRANÇOISE

Jacques—my letters!

JACQUES

Not right away! Wait a bit. We've so many things to say to each other first.

FRANÇOISE

We have absolutely nothing to say. Besides, your wife may come in at any minute, and I'm no more anxious to meet her than she is to meet me.

JACQUES

Sit down. She won't be here for at least an hour. And even then she won't come into this room.

FRANÇOISE

How do you know?

JACQUES

I told her I was expecting you.

FRANÇOISE

You told her that?

JACQUES

Yes.

FRANÇOISE

And she was willing?

JACQUES

Of course.

FRANÇOISE

Well! You have trained her properly!

JACQUES

Now, do sit down and tell me everything.

FRANÇOISE

But I've nothing to tell you. [*Sits on divan.*]

JACQUES

Oh! Come now! [*Draws up chair and sits near her.*]

FRANÇOISE

What do you want to know?

JACQUES

With whom are you in love?

FRANÇOISE

That, my dear Jacques, is my—

JACQUES

What do you care? I promise not to tell a soul. . . . Is it Moreuil?

FRANÇOISE

Perhaps.

Jacques

Seriously? Moreuil? Oh! but he's an awful looking fellow! [*He looks at her. She does not falter.*] No. You didn't protest. It isn't Moreuil. Then who is it?

Françoise

Heavens, you're impossible! [*She laughs.*]

Jacques

Ah! you're laughing—that's nice.

Françoise

I'm laughing because you disarm me. But, believe me, I've no desire to.

Jacques

You should laugh. It's very becoming to you. You're lovely when you laugh.

Françoise

I don't care to be lovely.

Jacques

What a fib!

Françoise

Do you think I care a thing about attracting you now?

JACQUES

Oh, I don't say that you care especially about it,—but you'd just as soon I thought you pretty. Well, I find you pretty, very pretty, even prettier than I remembered. Were you as pretty as this before?

FRANÇOISE

Jacques, please give me my letters and let me go.

JACQUES

I'll give them if you tell me with whom you're in love.

FRANÇOISE

I'm in love with no one.

JACQUES

No one?

FRANÇOISE

No!

JACQUES

Is it true?

FRANÇOISE

Oh! . . . I'd tell you . . . why not?

JACQUES

[*Thoughtfully, looking at her*]: Françoise? . . .

FRANÇOISE

What?

JACQUES

If you love no one, won't you—try to love me a little?

FRANÇOISE

You? Ah, no, I should say not!

JACQUES

Why?

FRANÇOISE

No, thank you! That's all over, fortunately.

JACQUES

[*Pause*]: Too bad—

FRANÇOISE

You think so?

JACQUES

Yes, it's too bad. . . . If you had wanted to love me . . . just a tiny little bit . . . I could have loved you so much.

FRANÇOISE

You?

JACQUES

Yes.

FRANÇOISE

You, love? Why, you don't even know what the word means!

JACQUES

Do you believe that?

FRANÇOISE

I know it. For you, love is an amusing pastime. It isn't your fault; you were born fickle.

JACQUES

I was born faithful, Françoise.

FRANÇOISE

Faithful to whom?

JACQUES

To you, if you wish it.

FRANÇOISE

And your wife, what about her? Are you already dissatisfied with her? Poor girl! How I pity her!

JACQUES

She isn't to be pitied.

FRANÇOISE

One year! Not even that—eleven months! Eleven months ago you married her, and already you're looking for an adventure. But then I was certain how it would turn out.

JACQUES

Really?

FRANÇOISE

When I read your note a while ago, I didn't have a moment's doubt. From the way in which you asked me to come, I understood immediately what you wanted.

JACQUES

And you came, just the same?

FRANÇOISE

Because of my letters.

JACQUES

True enough,—pardon me!

FRANÇOISE

But I knew perfectly well that you were thinking much less about returning them to me, than in seeing if I still loved you. I know you, Jacques!

JACQUES

Not so well.

FRANÇOISE

Oh, come now, it's so natural. After that long trip, you came back to Paris, and began getting bored. For a man like you, married life is terribly monotonous, isn't it? A distraction's almost imperative! Only, my dear Jacques, you were wrong in thinking me still available. Your Françoise no longer loves you! And that's that!

JACQUES

[*Pause*]: Well—never mind. . . . [*He rises.*]

FRANÇOISE

That surprises you, doesn't it?

JACQUES

What?

FRANÇOISE

That one should be able not to love you.

JACQUES

[*Sadly*]: No, it doesn't—it doesn't surprise me in the least, I assure you. It's the way things have been going.

FRANÇOISE

[*After a moment*]: Well, then?

JACQUES

Then nothing. I'm going to give you your letters. That's all. [*He goes to desk, takes out the envelope containing the letters and brings it to* FRANÇOISE.] They are all there.

FRANÇOISE

[*Looking at him*]: What's the matter? [*She takes letters and puts them in her lap.*]

JACQUES

Nothing.

FRANÇOISE

[*She rises and letters fall to floor*]: Why do you look so unhappy, all of a sudden?

JACQUES

Do I?

FRANÇOISE

You're not going to tell me that I've hurt you?

JACQUES

No.

FRANÇOISE

Then what's troubling you?

JACQUES

Nothing, my dear, nothing at all. I'm unhappy because—because we're going to part and will never see each other again, that's all.

FRANÇOISE

What do you care?

JACQUES

I shall miss you.

FRANÇOISE

Have you missed me much during the past year?

JACQUES

Perhaps—

FRANÇOISE

What a story! You would have told me!

JACQUES

How?

FRANÇOISE

You could have written me,—I hadn't forbidden you to.

JACQUES

That's true.

FRANÇOISE

Not a line—not even a post card—nothing! And still you expect me to love you. You must admit it would be too stupid of me!

JACQUES

It's never stupid to love. . . .

FRANÇOISE

It is to love you.

JACQUES

That's funny!

FRANÇOISE

What's funny?

JACQUES

How little you know me, my dear Françoise!

FRANÇOISE

Ah?

JACQUES

Really.

FRANÇOISE

Whose fault is that, then?

JACQUES

Oh! It's mine, I realize that.

FRANÇOISE

If you were capable of love, why did you never show it to me? Why did you always belittle the love I had for you? The day may come, Jacques, when you'll be sorry for that.

JACQUES

Be content, my dear, I'm sorry for it already.

FRANÇOISE

No, not yet. You're still too young. But—

JACQUES

You can't imagine how sorry I am, Françoise.

FRANÇOISE

Truly?

JACQUES

Yes.

FRANÇOISE

[*After a pause, looking at him*]: You're without doubt the most bewildering man I've ever known! Things happen when one least expects them, with you—and when it's too late!

JACQUES

Are you sure?

FRANÇOISE

Of what?

JACQUES

That it's too late?

FRANÇOISE

Of course.

JACQUES

Françoise. . . . [*He takes her hand.*]

FRANÇOISE

Don't—

JACQUES

Are you sure that way down, way down in you—there isn't a little flicker—that might be revived—by my being very careful? . . . Tell me?

FRANÇOISE

No! I don't want to!

JACQUES

Too bad.

FRANÇOISE

Where are my letters?

JACQUES

On the floor. [*He picks them up.*]

FRANÇOISE

Give them to me.

JACQUES

Will you do one last thing for me?

FRANÇOISE

What?

JACQUES

Since it's over, since we're going to say good-by and never see each other again,—let me kiss you.

FRANÇOISE

You're silly!

JACQUES

Please. I'd like, just once, to see your eyes again—

FRANÇOISE

My eyes?

JACQUES

Yes. Oh, not as they are now, not your everyday eyes. But the old-time eyes—the eyes I used to know— [*Going toward her.*] I want to see those eyes again—just to see them.

FRANÇOISE

No.

JACQUES

After that, you can go away. I shan't try to hold you, I promise. Grant me that one little happiness. [*He moves to take her in his arms.*]

FRANÇOISE

[*Resisting*]: No, I don't want to!

JACQUES

Please, please let me.

FRANÇOISE

[*Imploring*]: Let me go!

JACQUES

Françoise!—[*He embraces her.*]

FRANÇOISE

Let me go! I implore you! I don't want to— [*More feebly.*] I don't want to—I don't wa— [*Their lips meet. She abandons herself to him. The kiss, a long one, leaves her prostrated, her head thrown back on his shoulder, her eyes closed.*]

JACQUES

[*Looking down at her, in a low voice*]: How beautiful!

FRANÇOISE

[*Quietly, without moving*]: What's beautiful?

JACQUES

A woman!

FRANÇOISE

[*Releasing herself gently*]: I suppose you're happy now? You've had what you wanted? I was almost consoled, I had almost forgotten you. . . . And I had to come here to give you the satisfaction of torturing me all over again! . . . I don't know what I'm going to do. . . . And I knew what would happen, I *knew!*

JACQUES

[*Smilingly approaching her*]: My sweet Françoise. . . .

FRANÇOISE

Oh! no, no, don't come near me, Jacques, please! You wanted to know if you still had your power over me. Now that you've seen that you have, it ought to satisfy you.

JACQUES

Do you really believe that that satisfies me?

FRANÇOISE

You don't want to hurt me all over again, do you?

JACQUES

No, Françoise.

FRANÇOISE

Then give me my letters and let me go!

JACQUES

No.

FRANÇOISE

You won't give them to me?

JACQUES

I'll bring them myself to your house.

FRANÇOISE

No!

JACQUES

In a little while.

FRANÇOISE

You will not!

JACQUES

Will you be there at about five?

FRANÇOISE

No, I will not be there!

JACQUES

[*Tenderly*]: Yes, you will.

FRANÇOISE

But I don't *want* you to come!

JACQUES

[*Taking her by the arm and forcing her to look at him*]: You don't want me to?

FRANÇOISE

[*With less conviction*]: No—

JACQUES

Truly? You don't want me to?

FRANÇOISE

[*In a supplicating tone*]: No.

JACQUES

Françoise—! [*Again he embraces and kisses her.*]

FRANÇOISE

Oh! It's going to begin all over again.

JACQUES

What is?

FRANÇOISE

Everything, as it was before.

JACQUES

Not as it was before.

FRANÇOISE

Oh!

JACQUES

You'll see!

FRANÇOISE

It will be just the same, I know.

JACQUES

No.

FRANÇOISE

Why? What's been changed?

JACQUES

Me.

FRANÇOISE

Do you believe people change?

JACQUES

They learn a little.

FRANÇOISE

[*Smiling*]: While traveling?

JACQUES

Yes, while traveling.

FRANÇOISE

What do they learn?

JACQUES

To love the people of their homeland, the people who speak their language. It's tiresome to talk when one isn't understood. One wearies of it.

FRANÇOISE

[*Surprised, looking at him*]: Poor Jacques!

JACQUES

Don't pity me; I've come back to my own people.

FRANÇOISE

[*Leaning against him; tenderly*]: Oh! Jacques—it's terrifying! I already loved you when you were quite detestable; what will it be like if you start being a darling?

JACQUES

You'll love me a little more, that's all.

FRANÇOISE

[*Nestling against him*]: My dear one . . . I'm happy. . . . [*Pause.*]

[*The slam of a door is heard.* JACQUES *listens in surprise.* FRANÇOISE *starts. They separate.*]

FRANÇOISE

What is it?

JACQUES

Probably my wife returning.

FRANÇOISE

[*Nervously*]: Ah! I knew it!

JACQUES

Don't worry, she won't come in. [*They listen a few seconds in silence.*] You see? Does that reassure you? You can go without meeting a soul.

FRANÇOISE

[*Very moved*]: But—you're coming?

JACQUES

Of course I'm coming!

FRANÇOISE

Till you do, mv love!

JACQUES

Till I do, my love! [*He opens the door. She goes out, he following her. A few seconds later he reënters followed by* GEORGES.]

GEORGES

Madame asked me to let her know as soon as you were alone, monsieur.

JACQUES

[*Puts letters away. Annoyed*]: Well . . . go and tell madame. Then bring my hat and my overcoat.

GEORGES

Yes, monsieur. [*He goes out at right to* IRENE'S *room. A moment later* IRENE *enters.*]

JACQUES

Back already?

IRENE

Yes. [*She seems curiously disturbed and unnatural.*]

JACQUES

You weren't gone very long. Well,—what about the painting?

IRENE

What painting?

JACQUES

Praxine's painting—the one you wanted to buy.

IRENE

Oh, yes.

JACQUES

Didn't you bring it back with you?

IRENE

No . . . Jacques, I'd like to talk with you. . . . May I? [GEORGES *enters from rear door with* JACQUES' *hat and coat.*] Oh, are you going out?

JACQUES

Yes, but I have a few minutes to spare. [*To* GEORGES.] Put them there. [GEORGES *puts hat and coat on arm of divan and goes out.*] What did you want to tell me?

IRENE

I'll wait until you come back.

JACQUES

Please don't.

IRENE

I'd delay you. [*He looks at her and is struck by her appearance.*]

JACQUES

What's the matter with you?

IRENE

Nothing. I'll tell you when you get back.

JACQUES

No. Tell me now.

IRENE

It's not so urgent.

JACQUES

Oh, come, tell me—what is it?

IRENE

. . . Jacques, I'd like to go away—to leave Paris.

JACQUES

Leave Paris?

IRENE

Yes.

JACQUES

But what for?

IRENE

I'm just asking you to.

JACQUES

What does it mean? Where do you want to go?

IRENE

We might go for a while to Montcel. Father would be only too happy. He suggested it several times. All we need do is wire the caretaker. He'd meet us at Limoges with a car.

JACQUES

But why do you want to leave Paris? We've hardly been back a month!

IRENE

I know.

JACQUES

Why this whim?

IRENE

It's not a whim.

JACQUES

Explain yourself, then.

IRENE

I hoped—that you'd understand.

JACQUES

That I'd understand?

IRENE

Yes.

JACQUES

No, I don't understand.

IRENE

I mustn't—remain here.

JACQUES

[*Forcibly*]: But why not?

IRENE

[*Trembling all over, her head lowered*]: I've seen her again.

JACQUES

Ah?— [*Pause.*] Where?

IRENE

Praxine's. . . . She knew I was to be there. She was waiting for me.

JACQUES

How did she know?

IRENE

She knows everything.

JACQUES

Then she knows Praxine?

IRENE

She had met him once, in Vienna.

JACQUES

Did you know that?

IRENE

No, of course not.

JACQUES

So—you spoke to her?

IRENE

She spoke to me.

JACQUES

In front of Praxine?

IRENE

No.

JACQUES

What did she say to you?

IRENE

Oh!—I don't remember now.

JACQUES

You don't want to tell me—

IRENE

Really, I don't remember,—I was hardly listening.

JACQUES

She asked to see you again, I suppose?

IRENE

. . . Yes.

JACQUES

What did you answer?

IRENE

. . . That I didn't want to.

JACQUES

And then?

IRENE

She said—that she would wait.

JACQUES

Until when?

IRENE

. . . Until I came.

JACQUES

Isn't she going to Switzerland? [IRENE *shakes her head.*] Or is she cured?

IRENE

She says she doesn't care if she dies.

JACQUES

Don't worry, she won't die. That's the old story.

IRENE

She never lies.

JACQUES

Can't her husband take her away?

IRENE

They're not together any more. She has left him.

JACQUES

Really?

IRENE

[*After a pause*]: Jacques,—is it true that he came to see you a year ago?

JACQUES

Yes. How did she know that?

IRENE

She didn't tell me. [*Pause.*] It was after that, that she left him.

JACQUES

So much the better for him. Is there no one with her who could take her away?

IRENE

[*Shaking her head*]: No one. [*Controlling her feeling.*] She is alone—all alone—

JACQUES

[*After looking at her a while in silence*]: Ah! She's very clever—one must admit that! [IRENE *shrugs her shoulders.*] Mustn't she be clever to be able to upset you like this at your first encounter?

IRENE

How do you know that she wasn't more upset than I!

JACQUES

Of course, that was part of the plan! What surprises me, though, is that seeing you in this condition she should have let you escape, that she didn't attempt to hold you—

IRENE

Do you think—that she didn't try?

JACQUES

Well, then?

IRENE

To get away, I had to promise that I'd go to see her later.

JACQUES

[*Ironically*]: Splendid! [*A slight pause.*] And –do you intend seeing her?

IRENE

You know very well I don't.

JACQUES

Have you the courage not to?

IRENE

Yes.

JACQUES

It will be hard, won't it?

IRENE

[*Barely speaking the word*]: Yes.

JACQUES

How long—will you be able to resist?

IRENE

I don't know. That's why I'm asking to go away.

JACQUES

Well, then, go. Who's preventing you? You don't need me for that, do you?

IRENE

You won't come?

JACQUES

No.

IRENE

Why?

JACQUES

You want to know why? Look at yourself! You're breathless—your eyes are dazed—your hands are trembling—because you've seen her again, that's why! For a year I've been living with a statue and that woman had only to reappear for the statue to come to life, to become a human being capable of suffering and trembling! Well, I give up, Irene, do you understand? I give up! I've loved you more than anything in the world, you know that. I've proved it to you. As long as I hoped that some day you might love me as I loved you, as a man and woman can love each other, with body and soul, I accepted the rôle of your guardian. But now I've had enough. I resign from a useless and ungrateful task. Protect yourself, if you can. It doesn't interest me any longer. It's over! I'm tired of pursuing a phantom. D'Aiguines knew what he was talking about when he said, "Leave her alone, get out of her way, she isn't for you." He was right—Fortunately, there are women who *are* for us.

IRENE

Madame Meillant, for instance?

JACQUES

Yes.

IRENE

And I've tried so hard.

JACQUES

I didn't ask you to. It was you who came to me.

IRENE

Then you should have turned me away.

JACQUES

You shouldn't have said that you could love me.

IRENE

How did I know? I tried my best to love you! You always speak of what *you* have done! What about me? What about me? What about my feelings,—did you ever know anything about them? Did you ever give them so much as a thought? You loved me, it's true, but in your way.

JACQUES

Were you expecting platonic love from me?

IRENE

I expected a little more tenderness. Is there no spirit in love? Must it be only—*the body!*

JACQUES

Yes, you loathed that, didn't you? Go on, say it, be frank at least! [IRENE *lowers her head, and does not answer.*] But don't bother, don't say it! What for? I've known it for a long time.

IRENE

[*Without looking at him*]: Have you?

JACQUES

You wouldn't have thought so, is that what you mean? Well, you are rid of it now. You can breathe freely at last! I'll never impose my desire again. No more of that drudgery. It's over! Aren't you going to thank me?

IRENE

[*After a moment*]: Have you nothing else to say to me, Jacques?

JACQUES

No, really, I haven't. I think we've said all there is to say! Everything is quite clear, now. You can do what you like—I don't care any more. [*He takes his hat and coat from divan.*] Good night.

[*He goes out. She follows him towards the door. As it closes she utters a half stifled cry. Then she sits down, deep in thought, in a chair, her forehead resting in her hand.* JOSEPHINE, *the maid, enters from* IRENE'S *room, carrying some flowers in a box.*]

IRENE

What is it?

JOSEPHINE

Some flowers for you, madame, that have just come. [*She puts the box on the desk and opens it. It contains a large bunch of violets, like those in the first act.*]

IRENE

Who brought them?

JOSEPHINE

The florist, madame.

IRENE

Ah? [*Pause.*] Was there no letter with them?

JOSEPHINE

No, madame, nothing at all

IRENE

That's all, Josephine, thank you.

[JOSEPHINE *goes out.* IRENE *slowly turns and looks at the violets. She walks toward them, lifts them from the box, caresses them. Her eyes become fixed and hard. She turns toward the door through which* JACQUES *went out. She looks at the flowers again, seems to hesitate, then abruptly gets her hat, and rushes out to her room.*]

[*After a few moments the rear door opens and* JACQUES *appears. He closes the door as he enters. He slowly takes off his hat and coat and sits down at his desk, meditating. At that moment the outer door of the apartment is heard to slam.* JACQUES *raises his head.*]

JACQUES

[*He rises, goes to door leading into* IRENE'S *room, opens it, steps in and calls gently*]: Irene? . . . [*Again, louder and anxiously*]: Irene? [*He then reënters, looking surprised, and crosses hurriedly to desk, where he rings bell.* GEORGES *enters.*] Has madame gone out?

GEORGES

Yes, monsieur, just a moment ago.

JACQUES

Oh! [*Pause.*] Did she leave any message?

GEORGES

No, monsieur.

JACQUES

[*After a pause*]: All right, Georges. [*He sits down at desk.*] You can go. [GEORGES *goes toward rear door then seeing hat and overcoat on chair, turns.*]

GEORGES

Shall I take these away, monsieur? [JACQUES, *absorbed in his thoughts, does not hear him. After a few moments, he raises his head and notices* GEORGES *standing there.*]

JACQUES

What?

GEORGES

I was asking monsieur if I should put his hat and coat away?

JACQUES

[*After a pause*]: No. Leave them. I'm goin~ out, too.

THE CURTAIN FALLS

Printed in Great Britain
by Amazon

69081348R00163